Classroom, a teenage view

Foreword

Public education has been a cornerstone of the new Europe, an edifice that emerged from the ruins of the Second World War. In fact, until 1989, the attention paid to pedagogy could be seen as one of the few common traits shared by the countries of the former capitalist and communist blocks: in both cases, widespread access to free schools and the progressive extension of compulsory education were deemed crucial tools in order to form idealised citizens.

Amid the post-war period, a new human subject emerges across all industrialised countries: the adolescent, or teenager. This figure, which historically had never existed before, is no longer a kid, but not quite an adult. However, these subjects are formally recognised as adults when they turn eighteen (in numerous countries, around the late 1960s, the voting age was lowered from twenty-one to eighteen). Especially in the affluent West, this novel subjectivity spans the different social classes. Ideology, lifestyle and taste converge into an odd concoction of consumerism and rebellion. How to educate the vast masses of adolescents, and for what objectives, becomes a crucial issue across politics. It is no coincidence that just as the voting age is lowered, multiple countries opt to extend the timeframe of compulsory education. This is when the high school—which, until the early 1950s, was the site of reproduction of the bourgeois elites—truly begins to boom, and it soon takes on a focal, critical role in every young person's life. The 19th-century disciplinarian approach gradually loses its grip: it is first weakened by the deep contestation of 1968, and then newer experimental methodologies are introduced, aimed at improving collective education.

The project *Classroom*, made up of a variety of components—a travelling exhibition, workshops with high-school students, a dedicated digital platform, an international symposium, and this publication—is the result of a collaboration of three European institutions dedicated to architecture, arts and design.

The three participating institutions—namely Garagem Sul – Centro Cultural de Belém (Lisbon, Portugal), arc en rêve centre d'architecture (Bordeaux, France) and Z33 – House for Contemporary Art, Design & Architecture (Hasselt, Belgium)—rapidly found common ground for exchange, dialogue and collective work around the subject of adolescence and the spaces where teenagers are educated. Every worker for these institutions had similar personal experiences when younger: the memories of these formative years can be considered the collective mental substrata of all European citizens.

In the inception of this joint initiative, it became immediately clear that reflecting on the current state of secondary education was a necessary task.

Stimulated by the initial prospective ideas of the curator, Joaquim Moreno, we shifted our focus to the spaces and physical qualities of the sites that we studied. *Classroom* could be described as a vast deductive inquiry: by analysing and understanding multiple factors—such as the layout of the buildings, their presence within the urban fabric or against the landscape, their functional programme, the building materials used, the furniture, facilities and details—it becomes possible to read the intentions, not only of the architects and designers, but also of the educators, civil servants and politicians.

Through the case studies selected for the exhibition and this book, *Classroom* generated a kaleidoscopic portrait of the school setting within which millions of Europeans have grown up. The title of the project is almost a tautology, since it centres on the architecture of our most pervasive, obsolete and contested learning environment: the classroom itself. If we consider adolescence (and the oft-neglected spaces of secondary education) as the threshold through which children are transformed into the citizens of the future, the classroom helps us understand how learning takes place today, and how we might innovate in the design of secondary-school architecture. The project aims to identify and understand best practices, pointing out trends and solutions for the future, within a highly dynamic context where our access to culture and information is morphing at the speed of light.

The aim for this book is for it to become a reference in the ongoing debate about spaces of learning and education: it presents contributions from experts in the relevant fields, along with the research underlying the project, select case studies and testimony of the iterations of this initiative in France, Portugal and Belgium. It cements the optimistic view shared by the project's participants over the years: we all firmly believe that public education is a foundation of contemporary Europe, and that the right architectural and design solutions really can enhance and multiply its power.

André Tavares,
Centro Cultural de Belém / Garagem Sul Architecture Centre, Lisbon

Fabrizio Gallanti,
arc en rêve centre d'architecture, Bordeaux

Adinda Van Geystelen,
Z33 House for Contemporary Art, Design and Architecture, Hasselt

Learning
from the Classroom

Joaquim Moreno

Play—understood as the central priority of learning environments in post-World War II reconstruction—embodied the mutual fascination between progressive pedagogy and progressive architecture. What the Swiss architect Alfred Roth considered the most urgent and fascinating task for contemporary architecture, namely the construction of schools,[1] evidenced such a convergence. But the youth of all countries, to whom Roth dedicated his book, outgrew their childhood and became what would be the engine of the nascent consumer society (or the "age of affluence", as Tony Judt described it): that is, the TEENAGER.[2] The massification of secondary education transformed this new consumer into a new historical subject. Yet, the paradoxical site for the emergence of this subject was not an invention like the playground, and was instead the oldest and most widespread place of learning: the classroom. This is the setting for this research, the agonistic play between a new subject and an old place, observed in the rear-view mirror of the recent cycle of transformation, somewhere between CONSUMPTION and contagion.

Adolescence itself was one of the most disruptive and culturally determined inventions of the twentieth century, between the acquisition of literacy in childhood and the

1. Roth, Alfred, *The New School*, Girsberger: Zurich, 1950.

2. Judt, Tony, *Postwar: A History of Europe. Since 1945*, The Penguin Press: New York, 2005. Particularly section X of Part Two.

9

collective production of knowledge at university. So why does adolescence seem to languish in what we assume are obsolete environments that blur the borders between learning and normalising? Probably because change also changes, and is not always evident. In fact, schools' quick technological reaction to the Covid-19 pandemic was only possible because the classroom had already changed: it had become an obsolete hybrid, in the sense that it was no longer at the cutting edge, but that it worked and was widely distributed. Maybe the classroom had become an obsolete medium, following Marshall McLuhan's warning: "If it works, it's obsolete! Until a technology has existed long enough to permeate social psyche and sensorium, people can't really live with it."[3] And, like other obsolete media, it became the content of other socio-technical environments, mutating into software like Google Classroom. Also, most learning now happens via the protocols of the classroom, i.e. listening, assembling, experimenting or evaluating, not exactly through its material and physical constraints: today, the classroom is also immaterial.

This obsolescence and immateriality enabled the classroom to react quickly to the pandemic, which in turn made it continuous, instead of discrete and scheduled: it lost the synchronisation that previously bound the learning collectives in time. The classroom became pervasive, extending to the domestic space and to the life of the entire domestic community. It was as much a space as it was a node in a far more complex learning infrastructure, a portal to a much wider collective, a learning infrastructure for getting together, exchanging and networking, in a scale well beyond the unit of the school. This is a very different perspective from earlier debates, which proposed moving past the obsolete classroom and reconstituting learning collectives through larger and more agonistic common spaces, still inside singular purpose-built environments that are socially signified as schools. We learned that localised learning environments can be very efficient, and, conversely, that obsolete and widespread ones can be very far-reaching. The classroom is thus a medium like television: it is not too edgy, but it is everywhere, and mobilising

3. McLuhan, Marshall, "Understanding Magascenes", in *Print, America's Graphic Design Magazine*, July/August 1970, Vol. XXIV: IV, p. 20.

it as an up-cycled central node within a widespread network of learning environments is an alternative form of change, and a more feasible and ecological one.

The transformations of learning environments, as outlined above, are just one side of the story in a double spiral of change, given the ecological interdependencies between the protagonist of the age of affluence and their immediate habitat. The massification of cultural consumption cannot be understood without considering the tensions of the information shock and of the society of information, as brought about by electronic media. The movement of this ever-changing subject towards the present led to an ever more complex landscape, filled with new questions and contradictions: decolonisation, ecological crisis, rising inequality or new forms of illiteracy, demanding a more agonistic debate between pedagogy and architecture. There is no stable or widely shared notion of this particular subject, and a Google search for a definition of adolescence returns an important caution: adolescence is relative, and depends on whom/where you ask. Any inquiry about its cultural mutations, or how its form and age bracket have changed, are thus relative and contingent. In turn, this implies that we must be wary about projecting some version of our own memories, either as angsty teens or as demanding idealists. Maybe we need an update to the strange place between "Smells Like Teen Spirit" and *Fame*, where a generation came of age.

This situation calls for more dialogical forms of inquiry in order to study their mutual transformations. And, given the collective memory of an anxious time of autonomy without a voice, an adolescent perspective on the classroom must be heard and heeded. We need to consider all these contemporary reconstitutions and reorganisations of the learning collectives, as well as their spatial interactions, from a teenage perspective. That is, we must learn from adolescents, so we need to give them a voice, both individual and collective, and we have to listen to them: we need to dwell very carefully and actively on their thoughts.[4]

4. For the new centrality of learning in the school environment, see: Price, Cedric, "What About Learning", in *Architectural Design*, no. 5, May 1968.

11

We must engage these teenagers in an open dialogue, namely those who were asked to repurpose and domesticate the various layers of their electronic forms of networking/interaction for formal learning purposes. As soon as the lockdowns were over, these same teenagers came back profoundly changed: their worlds had been greatly reconfigured, but they returned to mostly unchanged classrooms and were expected to mitigate learning losses. This is the particular experience we propose to learn from, the perspective we want to capture, and the vastness of the world we want them to help us navigate. These learning processes needed questions before examples.

The emergence of adolescence as a new consumer category was fundamental for mass production and especially mass consumption, which called for a debate around the industrialised PRODUCTION of the classroom, not simply its material construction, detailing or management.

The end of bodily growth at the end of adolescence, and the role and place of these growing BODIES in many ecologies — both physical and socio-technical—was considered alongside research into the energies and flows that nourish and animate these individual and collective bodies.

The question of autonomy for teenagers, most of whom do not have political representation through voting, was the central question of the research. It was embodied by the theme of ASSEMBLY, which looked for parliamentary spaces and political process inside the school.

The transgressive nature of adolescence, with its fundamental defiance of limits, borders or social norms, was researched through the learning environments of artistic education, in the wide sense of performing, visual arts or music, mirroring TRANSGRESSION[5] in the experience of artistic freedom.

The final theme looked into those learning environments that prepare teenagers for the world of work and labour, not simply for higher education. In many cases, these environments simulate the obsolete or outdated working spaces of various PROFESSIONS.

5. hooks, bell, *Teaching to Transgress: Education as the Practice of Freedom*, Routledge: New York, 1994.

12

Exhibition photos in Bordeaux by Marion Parent and Lisboa by Tiago Casanova

Diverse classroom materials from various locations and time periods

This accumulation of furniture and equipment is an indication of the instrumental nature of the classroom. Its lightness and mobility attests to the way it evolves over time. This furniture is robust enough to withstand intense and prolonged use, and it also evinces the evolution of modes of sharing, sitting or paying attention. Leaning back on a chair, hiding under a desk, pushing two tables together, engraving a declaration of love or sticking a piece of chewing gum: these are all manifestations of the evolution of the bodies that use them. In a more overarching way, the table simultaneously encompasses the learning, the studying and the work of transition between childhood and adult life.

Harkness Table

This is a replica of the Harkness Table, an oval seminar table developed both as a material tool and as a teaching method for the private Phillips Exeter Academy in the 1930s, with the support of oil tycoon Edward Harkness. The learning environment it provides is very effective for small groups, but not very suitable for larger classes and frontal teaching. Essentially, it is suitable for the number of students it is designed for, but limits the possibility of other students being welcomed in. Perhaps by sitting face-to-face like this, without any hierarchy of seating, we can come up with other ways to produce good learning environments for all.

Empty circle

The absence of a table in the centre of a circle of chairs embodies a primary and very effective form of discursive assembly. Instead of the oriented and hierarchical space of the classroom, this circle of chairs is a small parliament, a meeting place for dialogue, debate and dissent. Designed by Hans Scharoun, these twelve chairs were loaned by Geschwister-Scholl under the condition they would be used for assembly, sitting together and debate, as an invitation to form a political body. The images of teenagers taking to the streets, occupying their learning environments and engaged in struggles for a better future, all reveal another facet of the classroom as a place to learn citizenship.

Growing table

A table on wheels, made to handle young plants or to bring to light the seedlings planted there. This functioning, and the small-scale ecology it embodies, is a metaphor for adolescence and the maturation it involves. The controlled environment of the greenhouse protects the development of the plants until they are strong enough to face the "outside world", in the same way that secondary school learning environments shield personal growth into adulthood. In that same classroom, there is a wheelbarrow step ladder to move and collect the fruits of the students' labour.

We contrasted this evidence of change with some contemporary mutations of the original questions, tracking the changes of the ideas that were guiding our research. PRODUCTION could also be about what kind of energy the classroom produces, or how the students participate in the production of their own learning environments. BODY could also foster further inquiry into local resources, understood as energy or matter, into cultural and technical practices of food production as learning subjects,[6] or the difficulties of making classrooms that are both healthy and sustainable. Teenagers are leading the fight against the climate inaction that is robbing them of a future, and their ASSEMBLIES have long left the buildings: their parliaments are taking the protest out into the street. The fight against normativity is TRANSGRESSING more limits, breaking the borders of the classroom, and challenging the norms of class, social organisation or neurological normativity. The process of emancipation, as encapsulated in the word itself, is mutating: it is now registering in other words and ways, demanding the work of self-actualisation that bell hooks urged for, searching for limits intended for protection rather than transgression. And work changes faster than education, so the shops of earlier PROFESSIONAL education mutated into office parks, multimedia studios or kitchens and restaurants.

These themes were indeed questions, and we looked for what we called "SEED" schools: this way, we could ground the research, trusting that the ideas we were planting would grow into robust trees not apparent in the seed itself, and that we could learn from their very slow explosion, to paraphrase Bruno Munari's much-quoted adage.[7] Trees are defined by growth, like our historical subject: this was a very important metaphor, because, like the trees, these schools are still growing, they are still alive and changing. They are witnessing and dealing with the much-faster transformations of adolescence, and they belong, simultaneously, to the present and to the archives. We looked at examples of European public schools that have been continuously in use since they were built post-World War II

6. Waters, Alice, *Edible Schoolyard: A Universal Idea*, Chronicle Books: San Francisco, 2008.

7. Munari, Bruno, "Albero / l'esplosione lentissima di un seme", in *Verbale scritto*, Il melangolo: Genoa, 1992, p. 14.

15

(just as adolescence itself was being invented as a new consumer group), as well as recent mutations from a multiple and global context. Having witnessed many changes over the years, these seeds allowed for multiple forms of inquiry, visiting and listening to today's students in the grounds where their grandparents stood as teenagers, capturing their voices and environments in moving images. More recent examples shed light upon the many faces and dimensions of adolescence, as distant as rural Burkina Faso is from downtown Los Angeles.

Architectural theory has long laboured under a fragile hypothesis about its ability to influence the course of things. Forms, after all, outlast uses or functions, and we realise by now that the desire to build new things for new uses whips up that storm called progress, which blows in from paradise and leaves a trail of devastation in its wake, all the way to heaven. It is a basic point to think that the greenest classroom is the one that already exists, and that the network of classrooms is a form of renewable pedagogical energy only if it is continuously shared and recycled, or, to put it another way, reinvented. Given that all these cycles, all these metabolic transformations, are embedded within the very flesh of buildings, the best way to learn about change is to learn from what already exists. Having kept or regained their original designs, and adapted to many pedagogies and inflexions of adolescence itself, these environments provided the traces, the subtle changes, we were looking for in this archaeology of learning. The main objective of the historical landscape and the contemporary inventory is thus to assemble a research laboratory that listens to the diverse and inclusive voices of adolescents, and makes them participants in the production of their learning environments.

The central commitment to learn from adolescence (that is, not simply to teach or learn about it), and make it the protagonist of the learning collectives, is a way of bringing this partially disenfranchised part of society back into the conversation. Getting a seat at the table is a form of participation and representation, and an opportunity to make these

16

Drawing tables and stools, canvas holders and score holders
The equipment used by the Aveiro Music School, mostly designed by Maria Noémia Coutinho, is adjustable. It adapts both to the bodies it supports and to the tasks it enables. It bears the traces of more than half a century of joyful inventions, adjustments and, above all, non-conforming uses, which are essential for student-creators who are asked to transgress their limits as part of their learning.

Work bench
As a replica of a learning bench found at St. Crispin's, this work tool represents the blending of the classroom and the workshop space. With a vice on each side, it organises learning by doing. It also testifies to the evolution from individual apprenticeship, subject to the mastery of the trade, towards a collective apprenticeship around a table in the shared classroom. This object is thus a lesson on the tricky cohabitation of work and learning environments.

socio-technical environments more equitable, inclusive and welcoming to the multiple diversity that they already embody. And tables are indeed the nodes of all these networks: taking a seat at a learning table is to be represented, connected and to belong.

The main conclusion of this archaeology of learning —researched through historical inflexions and present consequences, not through the lenses of the canon—is that the classroom is far more diverse than we had anticipated. It changes in very subtle ways, and some of these shifts can only be seen through the eyes of teenagers. We can look for turning points (such as technological incorporation, furniture, equipment, size or mechanical systems), but without a teenage view on the process, we would still be dealing with a very schematic fiction about how those learning environments really work, and a simplified vision of their learning subjects. The main purpose is to narrow the gap between how societies suppose that teenagers learn, and teenagers' lived reality of learning. This requires listening to other ideas and observing other shifts, and treating teenagers as autonomous cultural, social and scientific agents, with specific forms of exchange and collaboration. It also entails paying close attention, with curiosity, to their ways of imagining the present and the future. The non-hierarchical and multi-directional learning environment that most of them yearn for is unlikely to materialise fully, but it would certainly make for a more reflexive and reactive field, one more attentive to feedback and more committed to learning together.

Exhibition photos in Hasselt by Selma Gurbuz

Exploding Classrooms

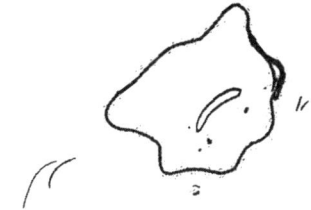

Joaquim Moreno
in conversation with Catherine Burke

JM   This book pays more attention to the EXPLODING
CLASSROOM than to the EXPANDING SCHOOL,
and it concentrates on the massification of adolescence and
secondary education. It questions the many ways in which
the very old classroom was exploding in order to accommodate
the invention of a very recent historical subject: the teenager.
And it also traces the reciprocal transformations and accommo-
dations of adolescence and the classroom, focusing on learning
environments that witnessed this shift and that are still changing
and sharing the present. Your work was a fundamental
companion in this journey, and we would like to go over your
thoughts about these changes and permanencies, and how they
project into the future.

   The image of a future built upon the ruins of progress is
today a widely shared horizon, and the school has increasingly
become the paradoxical place where we try to build an
undetermined and possible future. So, questions about the
future of the classroom arise.

Catherine Burke's work is a
very powerful rendering of
the educational landscape
of the last two centuries, in
both its physical and
human perspectives. Her
attention to the built
environment, to its types
and artefacts, sets the stage
for the drama of learning,
and Burke's sharp focus on
the many actors of the
learning process
— including architects,
policymakers, pedagogues
and students—brings it to
life. We tried to weave her
broad reflection together
with the questions raised
by this cross-perspective on
the changes of adolescence
and the classroom.

C B School has traditionally been caught between past, present and future, but perhaps it has been most concerned with preparing young people for the near future. There's a long history of declaring the classroom out-of-date and no longer suited to present needs. Early in the twentieth century, Frederick Sanderson, headteacher at Oundle School, a private school near Peterborough, England, believed that the design of spaces for learning and teaching required radical change. He believed that a school should be a microcosm of the world as we would wish it to be. He therefore set about reconstructing the existing school to remove classrooms, replacing them with spacious halls and galleries, workshops, laboratories, gardens, art rooms, libraries and museums. He believed that these changes would support active learning through inquiring, making and doing, and that they would help support cooperation, collaboration and engagement with the school's environment. Around the same time, but in the north of England at Prestolee, near Bolton, headteacher Edward O'Neill set about removing the classroom from his school, a standard primary school for local children. O'Neill also believed that children learn best when they are actively engaged in making and doing. He had the school pupils reconstruct the school using recycled materials from the former classrooms. This enabled learning through research, and it produced a school building and gardens that the children and local community were invested in. And it's not only in England; there are similar examples elsewhere too. In Bilthoven, in the Netherlands, for example, Kees and Betty Boeke started the Werkplaats school, where the maxim of learning through the head, hand and heart challenged the traditional sedentary nature of the classroom. All these examples, and there are many more, came about partly in response to the tragedy of World War I, when it seemed to make sense to reconfigure education, urgently, for the future. Actually, the same thing happened directly after World War II in many nations. Schools that were built in this period often emphasised, through their design, their crucial role in strengthening democracy and democratic processes. Envisaging a pupil who is free to move and exercise choice, and who can learn to rebuild the world in microcosm, required spaces other than the classroom box. So, the classroom of the future has long been considered to be emerging out of the ruins of the past, but it has strongly survived the challenge.

J M   What will be its form and its matter, and what energy will animate it?

C B   As an historian, I am aware of the rich history of radical experimentation and adventure in overcoming the "hegemony of the classroom"—an expression often used by the late architect David Medd—as well as resistance to it. Often, once the visionary headteacher moves on, the school reverts to the traditional model, like elastic. So, this is a matter of belief and conviction. It tends to be the case that strong state control of the curriculum and teacher training leads to conformity rather than experimentation. Today, the present situation is interesting. The pandemic showed, in many parts of the world, that learning could indeed happen anywhere and at any time, supported by teachers working remotely via internet platforms. This, in a way, undermined the significance of the classroom, and for those children and young people who were privileged enough to have support and space at home, and good internet connections, they learned well and at their own pace. But the vast majority of children, and their parents, realised the value of school and its familiar rhythms, and were glad to return to the classroom. Also, the specific and complex skills of teachers and the value of face-to-face contact were more recognised. So, while it is true to say that the classroom looks increasingly outdated, particularly when our attention is drawn to the myriad of ways that technologies can expand the spaces and places of learning, I'm guessing that the classroom and the school will survive as an institution that we recognise.

J M   How will it recycle and reuse existing spaces and protocols? And what will be its places, its communities, and its networks?

The shared uncertainty of environmental crisis and resource depletion appears to be engendering new bonds among teenagers and generating new forms of community and protest. Will they translate into new forms of equality? And into less normativity?

CB   The ongoing climate emergency suggests we should think very carefully before we decide to build new schools anywhere on the planet. Reconstruction and rebuilding may well be more sustainable for future uses, and the act of critically assessing what is there in the present has the capacity to engage present-day users and the wider community in determining what is necessary and what should change. "We rebuild our school", if well-conceived, has the capacity to engage learners, teachers, parents and the wider populace in reassessing the requirements for classrooms and other alternative spaces. Taking pupils' experiences seriously is vital if such a task is to succeed.

This process is demanding of time and skills, and it perhaps requires the shaping of a new kind of school professional: a specialist pedagogue of place, able to record and document how the school mattered in the past and how it can matter in the present and future.

JM   This fantastic new agent you propose, the specialist of place: how can it relate to environmental protests and the emerging voices of teenagers?

CB   The idea of a special pedagogue of space and place came from a combination of things. First, I saw an example of a school for younger children where a person had been employed specifically to work with the pupils on enhancing the outdoor school environment, integrating construction and creative endeavours with learning—a kind of enhanced caretaker. The school I visited is in Hamilton, New Zealand. Second, I was inspired by Colin Ward's suggestion that if schools really were to utilise and contribute to the local community, then this should not be a marginal activity, something rarely experienced: in fact, it should be at the heart of education for citizenship. For this,

24

Colégio Campo de Flores CCF

A memory from a high school classroom ...

Susana
Elisabete
Marta ——— Professoras
Carmen
Sandra
Alice

A memory from your high-school classroom...
Campo de Flores CCF School

25

Susana
Elisabete
Marta   teachers
Carmen
Sandra
Alice

Un souvenir de ta salle de classe au collège ou au lycée...

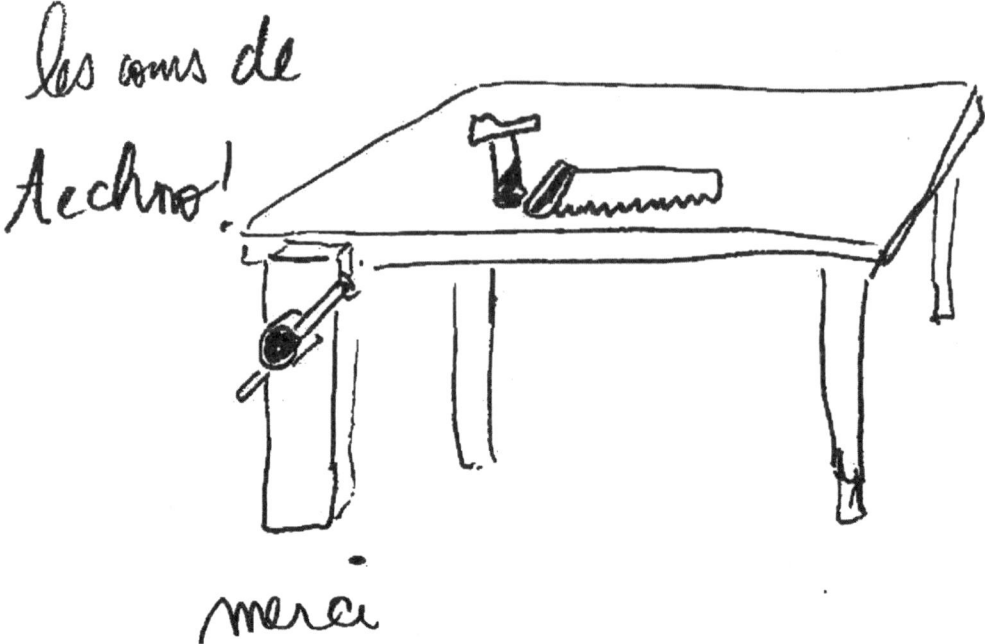

les cours de Techno!

merci

Où est cette salle de classe?

dans mes bons souvenirs rêvés

merci !!!
Thibault

A memory from your high-school classroom...
technology classes!
thanks

Where is this classroom?
in the nice memories
of my dreams
thanks!!!
Thibault

traditionally trained teachers were ill-equipped and needed support. Finally, teacher training needed to envisage the possibility of a new kind of pedagogue, possibly combining the talents of educators, youth and community workers and playworkers. These days, practically the whole of teacher training envisages the classroom as the primary learning space, unquestioned.

JM   Most of the massification of adolescence in the western world after World War II involved both the mass consumption and mass production of learning environments. To address the industrialisation of the classroom, we tried to visit and document functioning schools and interview current students about their perspectives. At St Crispin's, we suddenly plunged into the old debate between art and social service. We tried to frame this debate both from a productive and a pedagogical point of view, but you observed it through the eyes of Mary Medd.

How would it have appeared then, at the beginning of CLASP (the Consortium of Local Authorities Special Programme) and pre-fabrication, and how do you see it today?

CB   St Crispin's school in Wokingham, United Kingdom, is an interesting example of post-war school building. When it was built in the early 1950s, there already had been quite a lot of schools built in what is called the Home Counties—residential areas around London—but these had mainly been schools for younger children, primary schools. The task here was to realise, through design and construction, what a school for the older child who did not excel in academic subjects might be. It was envisaged from the start as a design investigation, and it was hoped that the results would demonstrate to others the possibilities of a progressive curriculum that engaged the head, hand and heart. David and Mary Medd believed that the elements of school design that formed the modern primary school were equally applicable here in a school for older children. That is why you see, in its earliest configurations, not the removal of the classroom exactly, but certainly a

27

modification. Originally, each classroom had its own adjacent work area, where it was envisaged that pupils would be unseated and engaged in experiments, modelling, making and design. But it was not long before the growing school population led to the replacement of these spaces by more classrooms. St Crispin's was a bold design and celebrated its confident early years through the incorporation of some exceptionally beautiful murals. Over time, however, the school ceased to flourish and came to be known locally as St Dustbins! The murals were painted over in an effort to improve its reputation.

The materials used in its construction were light and prefabricated, and they inevitably suffered wear and tear. CLASP schools were never intended to last more than thirty years or so. St Crispin's has recently undergone a refurbishment and certainly the murals have been restored by popular demand.

JM   How do you see contemporary debates about the production of learning environments, like user participation or the reorganisation of work itself?

CB   There's a strong consistency over time in what appears to matter to architects (and sometimes teachers) when designing schools. There's a pull away from the classroom box and towards more open environments, and then the reverse, rather like a swinging pendulum. Flexibility is the word most often used to describe innovative features of learning spaces: that is, the notion that a teacher or even pupils might be able to rearrange spaces by means of loose-fitting elements such as easy-to-move furniture and moveable walls. But if you take the long view, this debate about the end of the classroom box has been ongoing for at least a hundred years. Current debates on the importance of test results and the associated league tables, such as the PISA (Programme for International Student Assessment) studies, tend towards returning—if we ever left it—to the traditional classroom: here, pupils are arranged in rows, facing the black/whiteboard, and are seated for most of the day in rooms designated for specific subjects. Nevertheless, and despite this trend, architects designing schools today often seem to compete to see who can achieve the most open and most flexible of schools. Often, the idea of the 21st-century workplace or the technological revolution is used to deploy the argument that such flexibility is necessary to prepare young people for the uncertain future of work. This association between classroom design and the workplace is consistent too. Just think about the rows and rows of bank clerks, typists, seated factory workers, and so on, that were needed in the past. Today, and into the future, that world has disappeared, yet our ways of teaching and learning have not yet acknowledged the computer in every school pupil's pocket and what it represents.

JM The story about the murals is a good segue to bring up the pedagogical changes that occurred when the secondary modern schools became comprehensive schools. How was this pedagogical transformation remapped on existing schools?
CB If you mean, by this question, how did teaching and learning behaviours change by the introduction of comprehensive schooling in the context of the built environment, I think that the legacy of the secondary modern school had a long reach. Parents and the wider community understandably required reassurance that their children would receive a high-quality education. However, attitudes that had built up over time were resistant to the idea that the building they were familiar with could really deliver a good quality education in such a diverse school community. Even new buildings that were entirely comprehensive, with no legacy from a secondary modern past, soon became regarded as less desirable schools by the local press and communities. The role of the school building in this respect is critical: buildings release emotions. A well-ordered classroom in the public's mind is classically imagined— serial ranks of seated bodies, neatly arranged in rows; heads raised eagerly to receive wisdom. The opposite image, that of the disordered classroom, is disturbing. From the 1960s, such images of disorder in classrooms—particularly in the newly

29

created comprehensive schools—were broadcast on TV, causing even more disillusionment.

JM   We have the *Building Bulletin* (no. 8, 1955) in the exhibition, and the archival drawings exhibited were meant for publication, more than for construction. So how does it work, that thin line between a building that was mass-published in order to be industrially produced?

CB   The *Building Bulletin*, especially in the early years—the 1950s and 60s—was as much about attitudes to childhood and novel approaches to educational time and space as it was about construction. Education came first; the building followed after. In fact, the British architect David Medd, who was one of the main authors of those early issues of *Building Bulletin*, told me: "It was all about education: you started with the activity, then you thought about the furniture and then the different learning spaces, and only after that did you think about the building itself."

If you look carefully at the technical drawings in these publications, you find that the furniture and fittings are often carefully included. The bodies of children, i.e. their physical dimensions at different ages, are also included, demonstrating an awareness of the importance of comfort and of feeling that one belongs to a space. In these terms, I guess you could say that as well as being architectural texts, the *Building Bulletins* contributed to a change in the view of the child or young person situated in the school.

JM   Many experiments of exploding classrooms understood Environmental Education as a form of applied urbanism, a way to learn through the surrounding environment, mostly about the urban context. More radical projects like the Parkway Program, in Philadelphia, gave up altogether on a physical structure and tried to make the city itself the learning environment. The classroom is now exploding again, and the students are taking to the streets in protest again. What can we learn from

Uma memória da sala de aula na escola secundária...

Um professor infeliz que nunca encarava os alunos. Limitava-se a escrever, a apagar e a repetir o ciclo.

A memory from your high-school classroom...
An unhappy teacher who never looked at his students. He just wrote, erased and repeated the cycle.

Uma memória da sala de aula na escola secundária ...

Big windows to look at people in the library or the flying birds around the sky, small lockers to keep secrets and knowledge. The desk is tight enough to keep you from doing something big, but not tight enough to keep you sa used on the small amount of ideas you are supposed to follow relligiously.

Onde fica essa sala de aula?

In a place full of small but futuristic minds where half of them are not willing to select a lifestyle at the age of 17.

A memory from your high-school classroom...   32
Big windows to look at people in the library or the flying birds around the sky, small lockers to keep secrets and knowledge. The desk is tight enough to keep you from doing nothing big, but not tight enough to keep you focused on the small amount of ideas you are supposed to follow religiously.

Where is the classroom?
In a place full of small but futuristic minds where half of them is not willing to select a lifestyle ate the age of 17.

this early Environmental Education that might help us address the current ecological crisis?

CB   Protests are important in demonstrating young people's collective voice in challenging the slow response of governments and businesses to the climate emergency. What goes on in the classroom matters too.

Twenty years ago, with the help of *The Guardian* newspaper, I generated a large collection of children and young people's ideas around the theme "The School I'd Like". We received over 30,000 entries to a competition of the same name. With Ian Grosvenor, I produced a book reflecting on the results. It is full of terrific and practical ideas about what meaningful education might look and feel like. Here's just one example from a 17-year-old pupil from Manchester:

> The school I'd like would be open, in all senses of the word [...], the school would be much more integrated into the wider community. The notion of writing prize-winning essays on tropical rain forests without taking some action would seem strange. Schools would be part of the local and international community and would take part in solving some of its problems.

The school building featured greatly in critical appraisals of the habitual and familiar, and pupils from four to eighteen years of age produced imaginative sketches and even models of what might be in the future. The shape and feel of the classroom would be very much changed, and there was a plea for more contact with living things. "Let us out" was a cry, and many asked for more learning beyond the classroom—a school "without walls."

Such a sentiment characterised what you call early Environmental Education, and I believe you would find a consensus across national and continental boundaries in young people's ideas about a curriculum fit for the 21st century, not merely what it contained, but also how it is delivered.

As you say, in past decades there have been particularly radical experiments in replacing the traditional classroom model of teaching and learning in favour of directed urban wandering. This is true of the late 1960s, when projects like the Parkway Programme were run. Around the same time, architects and educators were collaborating in imagining their ideas for the future school. A very interesting example of this is found in the issue of the *Harvard Educational Review* (vol. 39, no. 4, Winter 1969) on the theme Architecture and Education. The front cover shows pupils evidently marching on the street, holding up placards. Inside, there are texts by leading architects of the time, envisaging education beyond the classroom and beyond the school. Italian architect Giancarlo De Carlo speculates on the imminent replacement of school and the return of education to the city streets. American architect Shadrach Woods considers the city as "the total school", and, as for the future, he declares: "education will become part of the physical milieu… no longer simple destinations in the systems of circulation, holes in the fabric of the public domain, but will form an essential part of those systems and that domain… The theatre of our time is in the streets."

The fact that these visions did not come about tells us how relatively conservative and limited the concept of the classroom is, as well as its utterly resilient nature.

JM   When researching the classroom as a political space, we found an incredible chain of student protests, linking Europe with South America, linking May 68 with the 2015 student uprisings in São Paulo, by way of the teenage protests against Pinochet's repressive regime and the "Penguin Revolution", which forged the current ruling political class in Chile.

Throughout, there is a chain of knowledge, there is learning shared through space and time, or, in other words, the effects of a classroom. Can you help us figure out this *de facto* classroom? And what about self-management? Like in the Lycée Autogéré de Paris.[1]

1. The Lycée Autogéré de Paris is an example of a self-managed public institution where students taken an active role in all of the school's decisions and activities, from the curricula to the food. See Aurita, Aurélia, *LAP! Un Roman d'apprentissage*, Paris: Les Impressions Nouvelles Editions, 2014.

34

CB   You are identifying some examples of pupil protest that appear to link young people across different parts of the world, through space and time. There are many more historical examples that get hidden in the histories we construct about past schooling. The question is, what part does the classroom play in these expressions of revolt and protest?

The school and mass education has always offered young people the potential and sometimes opportunity to collectively undermine existing systems. The physical containment of bodies in classrooms risks pupils becoming aware of their collective power. Treating the individual, rather than the group, helps undermine this potential solidarity. When pupils actively walk out of the school in protest, the container—the classroom—is breached, and that breaks the myth that societies hold onto, i.e. that all is in order behind the school walls and windows.

Whether or not there is knowledge and learning shared by pupils through space and time is another matter. Children are rarely taught their own social and political histories, but nevertheless act in ways that seem to suggest they are aware of belonging to what you call a chain of student protest. The historical record is limited, due to the failure of teachers to record uprisings against various forms of discipline. But it is clear from past and contemporary examples that the choreography of protest is learned from adult example. Often, adult campaigns and times of unrest correlate with young people taking action. So, I think it is more likely that pupils' political action responds to the wider social and political context of industrial unrest, rather than the existence of linked chains of knowledge. Of course, in the world of the mobile phone it is ever easier for pupils to organise actions, and this is set to continue.

On the question of libertarian school experiments and the role of the classroom, I would make the following observations. In these schools, the classroom tends to disappear, lessons are optional and much time is spent in larger spaces where collective decision-making, about the life of the learning community, takes place. I'm not familiar with the French example but I have visited the famous Summerhill School in England, some years ago. I believe that this school, established in the 1920s, has inspired other experiments in many different places. In such schools, pupils can decide whether to pursue formal qualifications, or instead they can explore their own interests, or do both. Much will depend on mentors, and the role of the inspirational and knowledgeable teacher is as relevant here as in the traditional school. These schools are fee-paying, so they mainly cater for youngsters who have resources and cultural capital to fall back on. This is not always the case for the vast majority, so such experimental schooling tends to work less in their favour.

JM   The position of the assembly hall in the two schools built by Hans Scharoun near Dortmund is quite telling in terms of how the learning subjects, the pupils, gather. In Marl, the central assembly is protected by the entire school: it is a gathering space for a school community composed mainly of young children. In Lünen, the assembly hall has a direct entrance from the street, and can be connected to the school's central square through a folding door. In this case, the assembly brings together the school with the wider community. Scharoun even calls this space, in some sketches, a "parliament". When we visited it, the building had been carefully returned to its original colour scheme, and the debates about singularity versus uniformity, and behavioural determinism versus democracy, appeared a bit off the point.

Do you think it is worth going back to this canonical building in order to reflect, again and anew, on the complex entanglements between notable buildings and changing pedagogical stances?

CB   From my point of view as an historian of education, with a research interest in the educational significance of architecture, I see Scharoun's work on school design less as part of the canon and more as part of a longer-term effort by educationalists to nourish the connections between home and school, between public and private spaces.

36

Un souvenir de ta salle de classe au collège ou au lycée...

Je dessinais sur les feuilles
de cours.

Ma tête est vide.
C'est pour ça que je suis en Art.

cursed

A memory from your high-school classroom...
I used to draw on my lesson notes.
My head is empty.
That's why I do Art
cursed

Uma memória da sala de aula na escola secundária ...

estudo do meio

A memory from your high-school classroom...
Enviromental study

This goes back to the ideas about breaking down the metaphorical walls of the school, as expressed by the American philosopher John Dewey in his book Education and Democracy (1916). Designing the school as a hub of community learning and development was taken further in the design of another "iconic" school, this time at Impington Village College (1929) near Cambridge, England. Working with the visionary educationalist Henry Morris, who at the time was regional director of education, Walter Gropius designed a school building that reached out to the local community; its ample communal spaces were designed for community as well as school use. Scharoun's school designs came after the war, in the early 1950s, picking up on efforts to strengthen democracy by means of educational renewal. It is interesting and pertinent to this conversation that the hegemony of the classroom was challenged in this reconfiguring of spaces for teaching and learning. Scharoun saw the break-up of the universal box-like classroom as necessary in order to support the individual development of the child. Rather than a series of identical classroom spaces that the pupil would progress through, he envisaged spaces designed to reflect his understanding of the child's needs at each developmental stage. The body of the pupil mattered, as well as meeting their social needs differently at various ages.

You ask whether it is worth going back to Scharoun's building today, and with it, whether we should revive his ideas about how our educational spaces may be designed to support the growth of the individual and the strengthening of democracy. It's a challenge, but the recognition of the diversity implied by his school designs should be embraced at this time when, in so many places around the world, democracy is once again in peril.

JM   We studied different agricultural schools, and most of them appear to be incredible ecological laboratories and very empowering environments dedicated to food sovereignty. Some places eat what they produce, and are open to community harvest. So why is it so difficult to extend this very active form of ecology to other high schools?

CB The problem is that despite various attempts over the years to establish equity and parity of esteem in the popular mind, in most cases academic achievements tend to be given more value than the vocational ones. This has, until now, reflected the world of work, where work with the brain is generally better rewarded in financial terms than work with the hands. Of course, these divides make little sense in many instances. So, in most societies in the industrialised nations, less social and economic value is attached to manual work and there is a misconception about how modern agriculture works, where new technologies are revolutionising farming. There are strong historical roots at work, as the Medds found out when they designed St Crispin's school; food education, gardening, cooking etc. were much more easily introduced in primary rather than secondary schools. And this continues to be the case.

The UK is preparing to introduce a new GCSE (General Certificate in Secondary Education) in Natural History, a qualification taken around the age of fifteen or sixteen. Work is currently underway to establish the curriculum, and one would think that learning outside of the classroom would be a necessary element of it —however, there is no sign, so far, of any consideration that part of the learning will have to take place beyond the classroom.

JM The research for the exhibition hinges, in fact, on politics and representation. That is why assembly is a central question, along with Scharoun's school, as an example upon which to build the dialogue. Other themes are arranged around this central one; opposite production, as embodied by St Crispin's, is labour, as exemplified by Jean Mermoz's professional school in Béziers. On the one hand, it's about how to produce learning environments, and on the other it's about how learning environments produce specialised workers and craftspeople, and also why, most of the time, such learning environments resemble the workplace. There is also an acknowledgment of the fact that these learning environments normally outlast the type of work whose apprenticeship they offer, as is the case of the Mermoz school, which is now a modernist icon that the students learn to brand, or the Bexley Business Academy, designed by Norman Foster for the kind of office work that is also likely to disappear. The question would thus be: how can learning and working environments be related in a transformative manner?

CB   Of course, a lot of learning takes place in the workspace and always has done, just as a lot of work has taken place and continues to take place in the home. Since the introduction of the modern school, the world of work and the world of education have been separated—and, with that, the boundaries between child and adult have been drawn and defined. Looking back in time, these boundaries have been drawn in different ways; they are never universal, and are subject to change.

JM   Another way to frame this question would be to address new professions and new forms of work, along with the dramatic digitalisation of work and life. Symmetrically, there is also a return to crafts and manual work.

CB   It's interesting that you've picked up on a return to crafts and manual work. There is evidence that young people today are not only digitally highly skilled, but, rather surprisingly, also drawn towards analogic lifestyles. It is not necessarily either/or. This is often overlooked by older generations who assume otherwise. An example that illustrates this well is a contemporary educational project in North Wales where volunteers, mainly young people in their first decade after leaving school, come together from many places in the world to learn how to construct buildings, make and decorate furnishings and fittings, and grow their own food. To do this, they draw on pre-modern forms of construction, as well as art and crafts local to the area, utilising traditional materials and tools. The work is slow-paced and practical. The classroom is absent, and learning takes place through collaboration and conversation on site, wherever the

41

Un souvenir de ta salle de classe au collège ou au lycée...

Ce n'est pas une salle de classe,
mais une "niche" près du
CDI. Le lycée était
dans un ancien hôpital
et le CDI dans la chapelle.
Nous avons passé des heures
suspendues dans cette salle
au dessus des couloirs
du lycée.

A memory from your high-school classroom...
It isn't a classroom but a "niche" close to the school library. The school was in a former hospital and the library in the chapel. We spent hours up there in this room, above the school's corridors.

work needs to be done. In the pedagogy, hierarchies are ignored: teachers and learners are hardly distinguishable from one another. This example teaches us several things: young people, who are skilled users and developers of digital technologies, are still drawn to the making of things that are honest, tangible, pleasing to the eye and lasting. They partake in activities that meet fundamental requirements for shelter, warmth, nutrition, community and culture. They can envisage future generations enjoying the fruits of their labours. This suggests a longing for an education that is designed not only to address individual needs, but also one that generates the collective enrichment of generations yet to be born. The slow pace of making and growing reflects an aesthetic delight in both the process and product. This suggests the possibilities of designing an educational process that allows time for the full engagement of all the senses in nurturing educational communities and environments, be they neighbourhoods, cities or schools.

J M   We inquired into artistic education, looking for some transgressive impulses. Following bell hooks' breakthroughs about transgression as a practice of freedom, we talked with teenagers from different geographies and with a range of learning interests, assuming that transgression was still a central point of the adolescent experience. But we noticed that the word did not register with the intensity we had expected, and we couldn't work out whether it was simply an erosion of the word itself, or a reduction in the role of counter-images and counter-narratives in contemporary self-invention. What is your feeling about the new ways teenagers confront edges, borders and social norms? What words can we add to this debate?

C B   Of course, we cannot generalise about the experience of teenagers, but what they continue to confront, across many national boundaries, is the popular assumption that they are somehow programmed to transgress. It is interesting that in your encounter with a range of teenagers that they did not register with the word or concept of "transgression". Arguably,

43

these days societies place greater emphasis on acquiring qualifications for a future of work that is changing so fast that it is difficult to grasp. This undoubtedly has an impact on teenagers' self-identities.

If this is partly about language, then the kind of words we might consider relevant to this debate are linked to definitions of young people's mental health and wellbeing. It seems to me that there is a kind of transgression at play in the new vocabulary of mental health. Words like "stress", "anxiety", "meltdown" and "depression" are far more widely used today than in the past, and are probably found to be more meaningful to contemporary teenagers. The classroom, in the context of these wider social expectations, can be seen to contribute in no small measure to this development. However, the classroom is so ubiquitous that it seems, as ever, to be a neutral container without agency.

JM   The exhibition brings together a wide range of learning equipment, focusing on the table as the main learning interface, more so than the screen or the board. From the work bench, drafting table, growing table, or even the famous Harkness table, we utilised the table, in its multiple shapes and protocols, as an index of the diversity and transformation of the classroom. Is this still a relevant metaphor, between the sharing of food and the sharing of knowledge, between nourishment and learning? Or are we headed to a time when we will eat and learn alone, at our own individual tables?

CB   It's good to focus on the table, also known as the workbench or desk. It's interesting how all three of these words promote a specific emotional response. "Table" implies a place of gathering, possibly for sharing food together or a place for display. "Workbench" brings to mind active learning and often a standing posture. "Desk" is certainly for sitting at. Changes over time in the design of school furniture tell us much about pedagogical attitudes and expectations of learning behaviours. Hence the shift from 19th-century galleries to benches holding lines of pupils, then to desks in pairs, then individual desks with attached seating. When group work was envisaged, lightweight and easy-to-move furniture was found to be necessary. In a London secondary school that I know of, one that experimented with group learning, bespoke six-sided tables were brought in to suggest that groupings of six pupils were expected to collaborate in their learning tasks. What is the future of the table in the classroom? Well, if we are serious about supporting diversity in our young student communities, we have to introduce as much variety as possible. Furniture, supporting body and mind, is essential and generally overlooked in educational environments. As David Medd and John Kay said long ago, in words that still ring true: "If school life is the starting point, the furniture and its disposition for that life must be the first step in the design process—not the last." (*The Architects' Journal*, February 1965)

© Aurélio Vaz

Production

The transformations brought about by post-war reconstruction and demographic growth required a massive expansion of the secondary education system, and prefabrication would play a decisive role in achieving this. The scale and urgency of the undertaking often dictated solutions inspired by industrial processes, leading to experimental educational facilities that were designed to be systematically replicated. St Crispin's School in Wokingham, built in 1953, is proto-typical of this approach: it showed how to bring down costs and cut building times by using industrial materials. The modularity of the prefabricated structure meant that traditional classrooms could be joined by more open workspaces, designated for hands-on learning.

It was made for war efforts, but it was never used. I know in the school there's obviously a lot of panels, and that's potentially why it's architecturally interesting... but if you're asking me, it's yellow...

an't imagine my grandparents being here because they're, I don't know, they're not really...
uppose they would have been here in a much different environment than we are.
much more different lifestyle in the end. With the gender stereotypes of women cooking and cleaning and men doing all the work. I just don't... I
nk my grandparents didn't even go to school, they just worked in a farm. So, I can't really imagine them going here.
grandparents started working when they were fourteen, so I don't think they had much time at school.

I mean, we know it's quite old and it's been here for a very long time and they're not allowed to knock it down, so it must be important.
When you want double doors... you can't have double doors.

© Aurélio Vaz

just feels like the people who built this school built a home for you. An
ternative place for you to feel safe and talk to friends. It makes you
el welcome despite your past or anything about you...

St. Crispin's School
Mary Crowley and David Medd
Wokingham, Berkshire, United Kingdom, 1951–53

d buildings, you usually think of like big and cold and... made of stone, but this, compared to those, looks quite modern.
nd I think that's why it's quite a revolutionary sort of thing. This building was built for practicality, not beauty. So, it's...
t... conventional. It's
piece of art.

This secondary modern school in Wokingham was designed by Mary
Crowley and David Medd, who worked on the UK Ministry of Education's
technical team. The school is a demonstration of the use of industrial
and prefabricated construction methods as a way to produce learning
spaces devoted to new pedagogical models, following the rolling-out of
secondary education to the entire adolescent population. The school
juxtaposed the conventional curriculum (hosted in a central building
containing classrooms stacked up to five storeys high) with its new
programmes (including a multi-purpose space and classrooms for
domestic science and workshops), distributed across modular and
expandable ground floor wings. The whole production process of this
school — design, execution, budget and schedule — was monitored and
documented in several issues of the British magazine *Architects'
Journal*,[1] and was publicly showcased in *Building Bulletin* (no. 8, 1955),
a publication of the Architects and Building Branch of the Ministry of
Education (the archival materials selected for this book were specially
prepared for this publication).

After several educational cycles had passed through the school, its
murals depicting the seasons of the year were erased. They had
represented the schematic pedagogical segregation between conventional high schools — through which students could gain access to
university-level education — and the localism of this other type of
secondary modern school, which was instead tasked with preparing
students for work, as well as reinforcing gender roles of significant
social immobility. Nevertheless, the school continued to change,
growing as it did through updated versions of its production processes.
And when the building was listed as a heritage site, its murals — and
the complex memory they entail — were restored. The greenhouse for
instructing farmers was transformed into music studios; the kitchens of
the domestic science classrooms are now rooms for studying ecology
and food; the workshops now have computers, and the textile classes
have shed their gendered stereotypes. Meanwhile, the ecological
problems of a building at the limit of its useful life — with single-glazed
windows, and without any lifts — have now also become a common
concern for the whole learning community.

I think the school is
good. It has a good
flow; if you go outside,
there are all these
different paths you
can take, which means
that some days, me
and my friends, we
just take a stroll
outside cause it's hot.
You go and buy some-
thing and just talk. The
flow is really nice in
this school. You can go
to places fast. You
have different areas
for everything, so like
French would be in
this place, you can
characterise every-
thing in this school.

1. Stillman, John and Eastwick-Field, John, MOE Development Work,
Wokingham, in *The Architect's Journal*, October 16, 1952; December 4,
1952; January 8, 1953; March 12, 1953; May 28, 1953, and July 23, 1953.

© Aurélio Vaz

REC TC: 00:32:32:10

We get all our food from Cuccina, which is our restaurant company. It's like an external company. And we have two options: the restaurant, which is the main place we do have to eat, and then we also have the street kitchen, which is sort of like a café. There's nowhere to sit there, but you can take it anywhere.

We're actually trying to work up a carbon footprint for our restaurant. That's one of our things as part of the School Council.

We do have a green team within the school, working to improve the environment side of the school. Making it more energy efficient and they have loads of projects going on. But they basically used to run around saying: "lights off!"

We even try small things in this school to help the environment, like we can have different kinds of cladding, and with Mr Hudson we're using an infrared camera and we're trying to find out where the heat is lost during school, and you see it's actually in the windows. We're losing so much heat because they're single-glazed windows. So, we're trying to find a way around that, like different sheeting on windows that wouldn't affect the aesthetics of the school in the way it looks. And it would still be a great listed building. Just, anyway, to reduce heat loss to save energy within this school.

building like the new science block is really energy efficient. It has really good insulation, the windows are double-glazed (I think), it has underfloor heating, which is much more efficient than central heating, a radiator system as well, and you've got solar panels on top of the science block. And it's just far more energy efficient than something like this, and we're trying to see if we can save energy on those areas as well.

Everyone has a voice in this school, really. It's just how to express that voice. There are different ways. So, we are obviously the head team. If anyone has any problem or any queries, they can pass it to us and we will pass it on, but we also have Student Council, which is the main body of the students, representatives from each form and they express their ideas from what their classmates are telling them. So, everyone has a voice in the school.

's just like a big weight; the older generations didn't have to think about energy and the environment and what effects was having. They didn't have to worry about their environment dying and having to go through the consequences. It's a tle bit harder on us, a big weight, and we have to think about it.

Each generation gets more and more woke and more understanding of other people. There have been, obviously, some not-as-good things that have come with time. But as people and as a society, I think we are changing and for the better, but I guess there's some people who just refuse to keep up with it.

52

There is a place that you can talk about these things. In School Council, we take on our peers' ideas (of course we must filter out the silly ones) but we get them to tell us the ideas they have to improve the school and then we take them to these meetings, and we talk about them. And a lot of the time they do happen! It's not one of those things where people say: "You have a voice, use it!", "Tell us what you want". And then it never happens. It's not like it here.

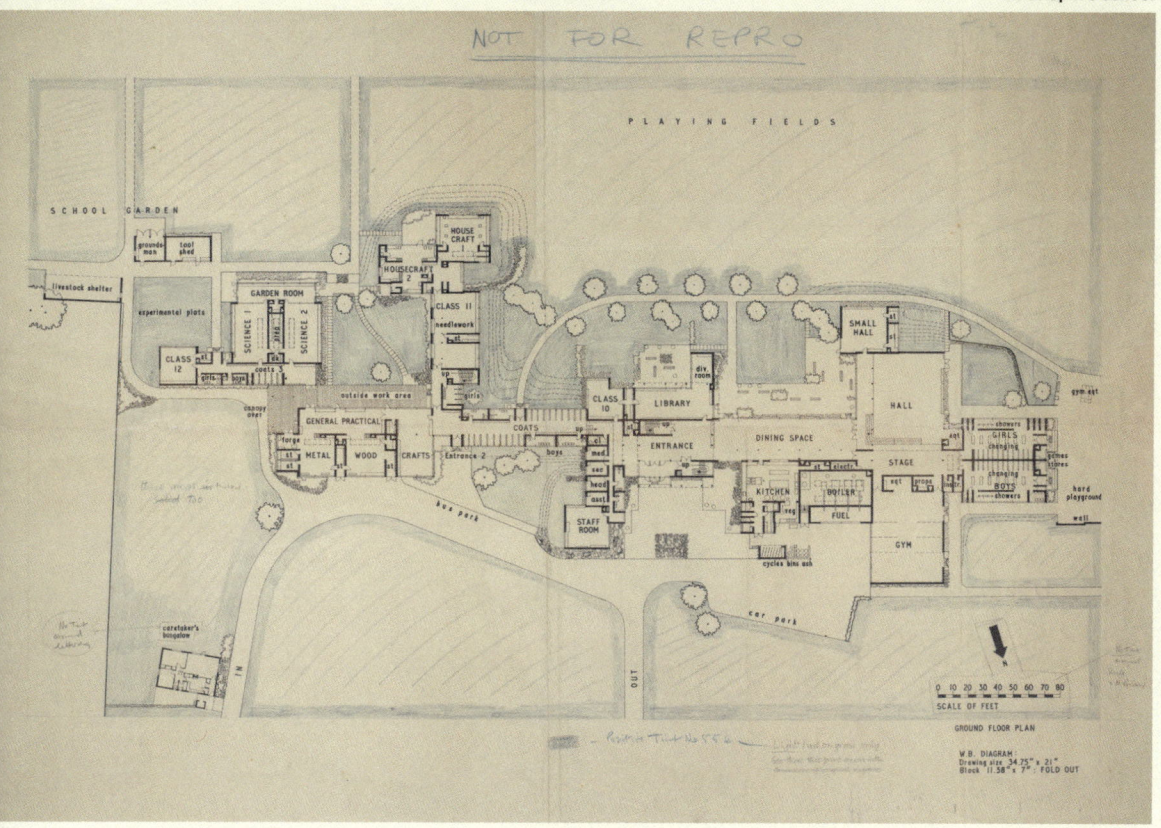

I think school, I mean our school, definitely prepares us, because we have the whole package, like the ethos. We have a lesson every Monday which is, you learn things that aren't in the classroom, like taxes and things you'd need to know... saving money, finance talk... just general life skills.

And we're very heightened with the fact that
this is something we're going to have to face i
the future. And this is with everything, like
global warming and sexism and racism and
homophobia. We're the first generation who
has really gotten properly upset about it, and
has really realised what it means, and what it's
going to mean for our future and now we are a
that age we're teenagers, young adults
entering society and... we have a voice... and
we have a voice now.

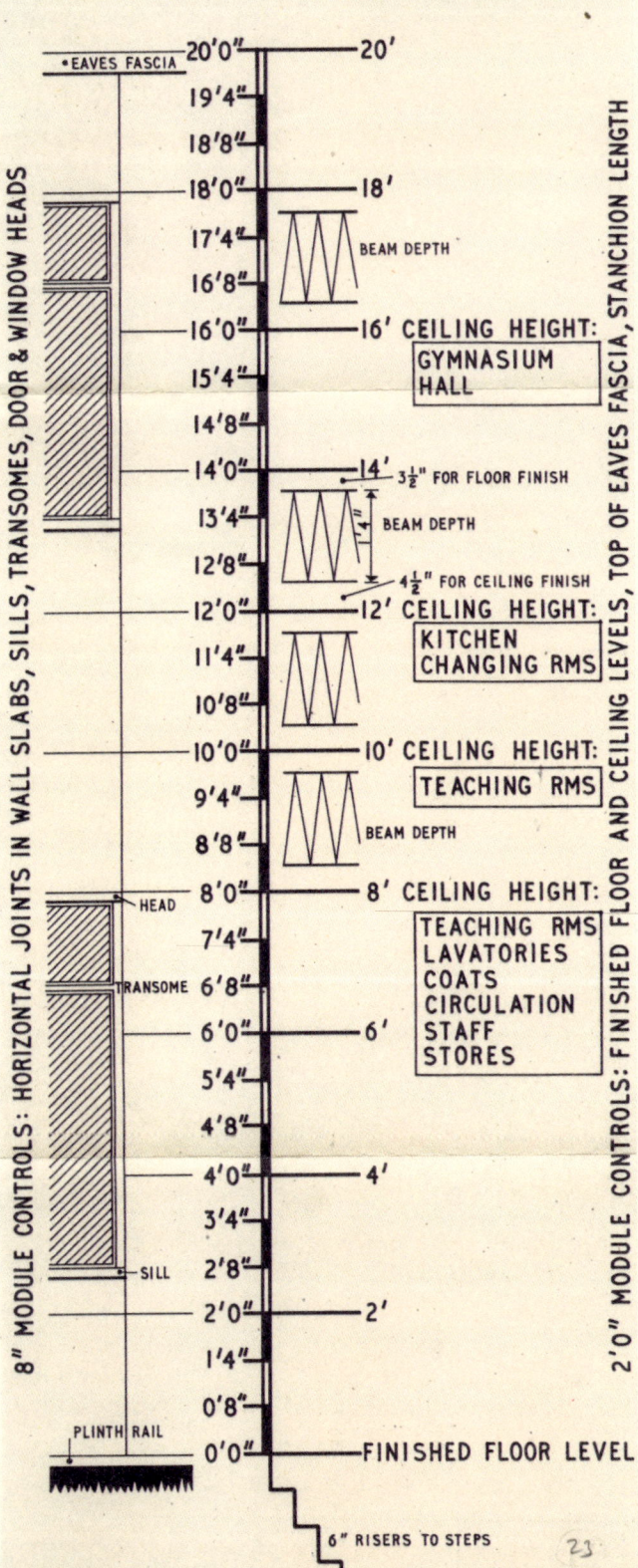

8" MODULE CONTROLS: HORIZONTAL JOINTS IN WALL SLABS, SILLS, TRANSOMES, DOOR & WINDOW HEADS

2'0" MODULE CONTROLS: FINISHED FLOOR AND CEILING LEVELS, TOP OF EAVES FASCIA, STANCHION LENGTH

• EAVES FASCIA

20'0" — 20'
19'4"
18'8"
18'0" — 18'
17'4"   ╱╲╱╲╱ BEAM DEPTH
16'8"
16'0" — 16' CEILING HEIGHT:
15'4"   GYMNASIUM
              HALL
14'8"
14'0" — 14' 3½" FOR FLOOR FINISH
13'4"   ╱╲╱╲╱ BEAM DEPTH
12'8"   ╲╱╲╱╲ 4½" FOR CEILING FINISH
12'0" — 12' CEILING HEIGHT:
              KITCHEN
11'4"   CHANGING RMS
10'8"   ╱╲╱╲╱
10'0" — 10' CEILING HEIGHT:
9'4"   TEACHING RMS
          ╱╲╱╲╱
8'8"   BEAM DEPTH
8'0" — 8' CEILING HEIGHT:
              TEACHING RMS
7'4"   LAVATORIES
              COATS
HEAD
6'8" TRANSOME   CIRCULATION
6'0" — 6'   STAFF
              STORES
5'4"
4'8"
4'0" — 4'
3'4"
2'8" SILL
2'0" — 2'
1'4"
0'8"
PLINTH RAIL
0'0" — FINISHED FLOOR LEVEL

6" RISERS TO STEPS   23

In the sixth year there's a lot more in classes, there's a lot more debate, and you are asked for your opinion, and you are asked to challenge if you don't agree with something, because that is how you can extend your learning and kind of express yourself. I think that's important.

Most of us already have part-time jobs. And then there's a difference between a job and a career, definitely. But I do feel prepared, mostly because of our sixth form education, as opposed to my lower school. You don't just learn the curriculum, you learn how to become a person, in a way. It sounds like a very weird thing to say, but you develop all those skills alongside, when you're learning in classrooms and then in sixth form you just fine-tune it to target whatever you want in life. So, we look at applying to universities, how to behave in the workplace, and the whole idea of having a uniform is to prepare you for work.

I think that's definitely encouraged throughout the school, to question what you are being taught, because how can you truly understand it if you're not questioning every aspect of it. If you stood up and accept what anyone is telling you, are you really going to learn it, are you really going to understand it?

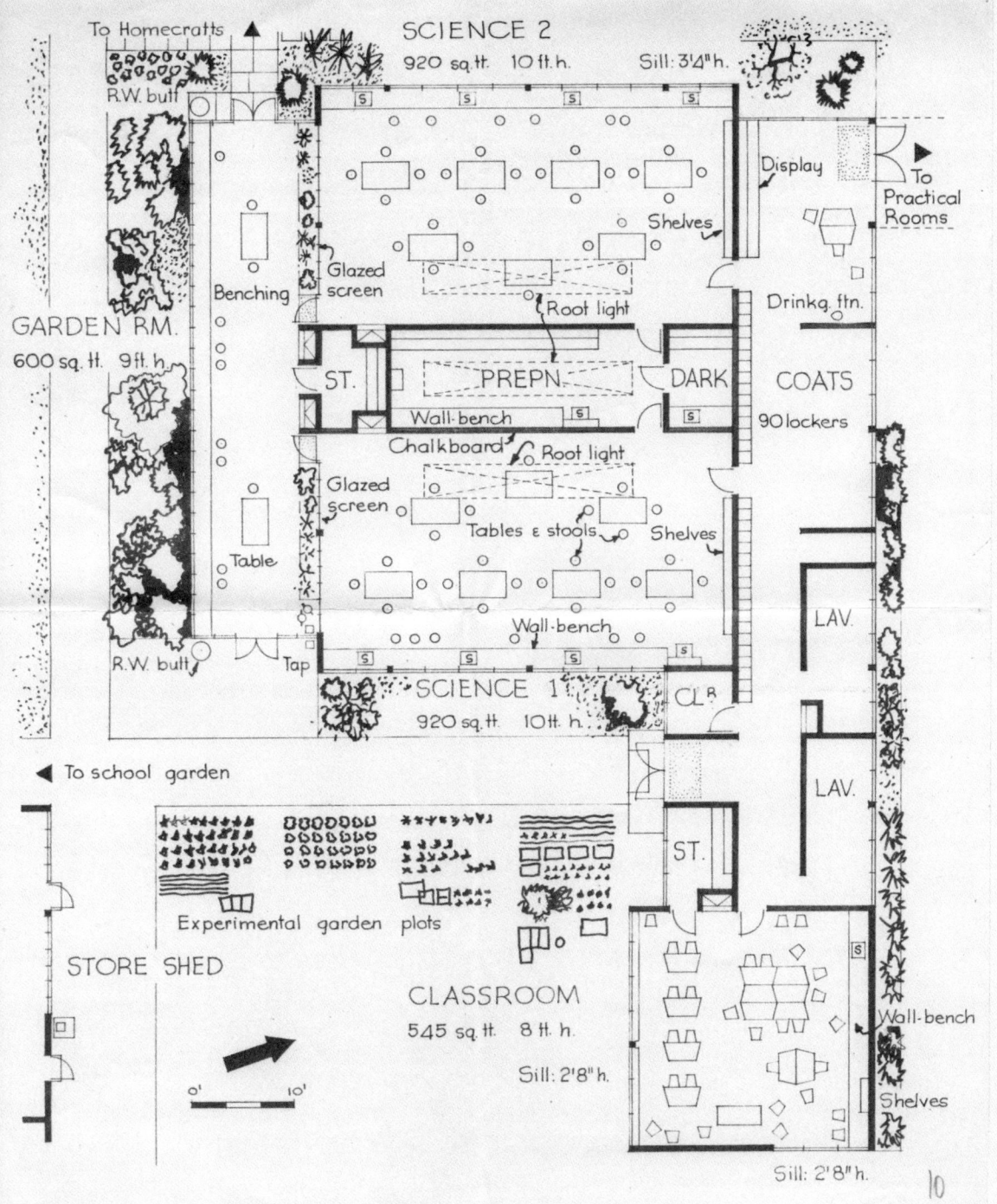

To Homecrafts

R.W. butt

SCIENCE 2
920 sq. ft.   10 ft. h.   Sill: 3'4" h.

Display

To Practical Rooms

GARDEN RM.
600 sq. ft. 9 ft. h.

Benching

Glazed screen

Root light

Shelves

Drinkg. ftn.

Table

ST.   PREPN   DARK   COATS
                                    90 lockers
Wall-bench

Chalkboard   Root light

Glazed screen

Tables & stools   Shelves

Wall-bench

R.W. butt   Tap

SCIENCE 1
920 sq. ft. 10 ft. h.

CL R

LAV.

LAV.

To school garden

Experimental garden plots

STORE SHED

ST.

CLASSROOM
545 sq. ft.   8 ft. h.
Sill: 2'8" h.

0'   10'

Wall-bench

Shelves

Sill: 2'8" h.

57

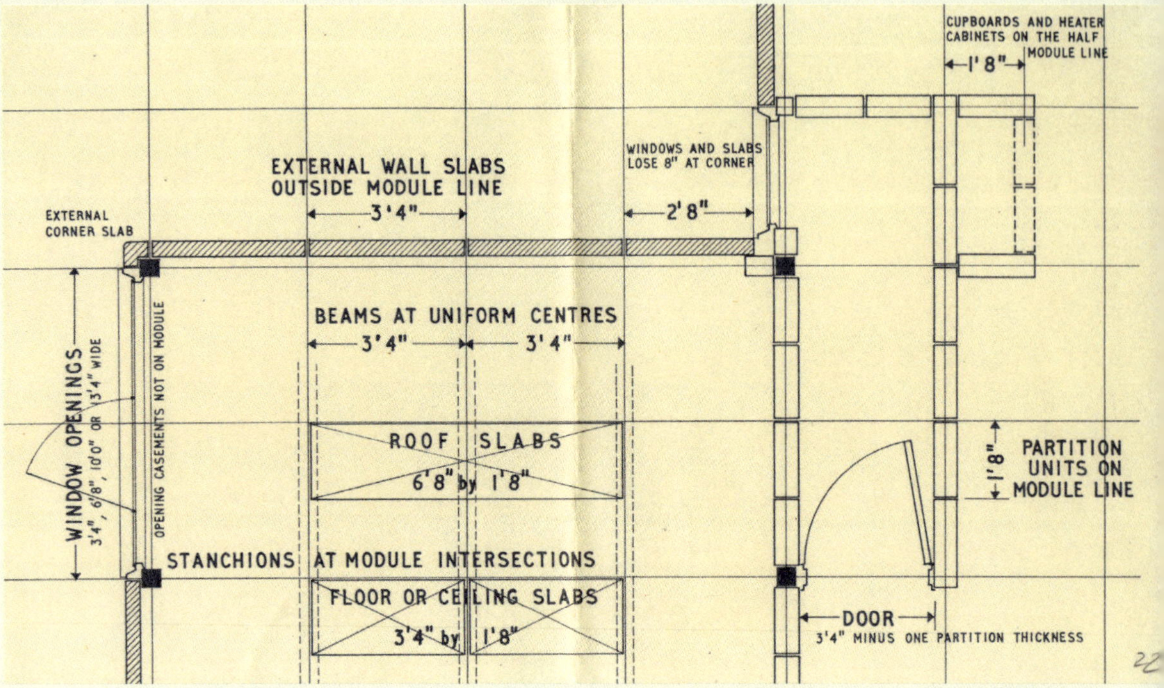

CUPBOARDS AND HEATER
CABINETS ON THE HALF
MODULE LINE

|← 1'8" →|

EXTERNAL WALL SLABS
OUTSIDE MODULE LINE
|← 3'4" →|

WINDOWS AND SLABS
LOSE 8" AT CORNER
|← 2'8" →|

EXTERNAL
CORNER SLAB

WINDOW OPENINGS
3'4", 6'8", 10'0" OR 13'4" WIDE

OPENING CASEMENTS NOT ON MODULE

BEAMS AT UNIFORM CENTRES
|← 3'4" →|← 3'4" →|

ROOF SLABS
6'8" by 1'8"

↑ 1'8" ↓
PARTITION
UNITS ON
MODULE LINE

STANCHIONS AT MODULE INTERSECTIONS
FLOOR OR CEILING SLABS
3'4" by 1'8"

DOOR
3'4" MINUS ONE PARTITION THICKNESS

22

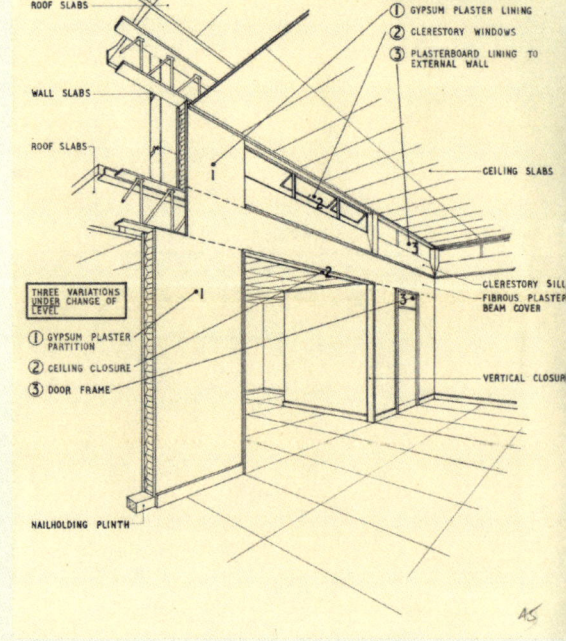

THREE VARIATIONS OVER
CHANGE OF LEVEL
① GYPSUM PLASTER LINING
② CLERESTORY WINDOWS
③ PLASTERBOARD LINING TO
   EXTERNAL WALL

ROOF SLABS

WALL SLABS

ROOF SLABS

CEILING SLABS

CLERESTORY SILL
FIBROUS PLASTER
BEAM COVER

THREE VARIATIONS
UNDER CHANGE OF
LEVEL
① GYPSUM PLASTER
   PARTITION
② CEILING CLOSURE
③ DOOR FRAME

VERTICAL CLOSURE

NAILHOLDING PLINTH

AS

I suppose you see that in the school as well.
We're now a fully mixed school. We've got
different people doing different things. I'm
doing textiles, I'm in year ten and I am a man,
and there are people doing different subjects
that potentially could be seen more as a
woman's role. Or a man's role…

Participation and Production: Building Site and Seminar Table

What should the production models of learning environments be? Should they be typified and prefabricated, or should they all be unique, but based on the available local knowledge and materials? And what is the best way to actively listen to the diverse and inclusive voices of adolescents, and make them participants in the production of their own learning environments? How can this partially disenfranchised part of the citizenry be brought back to the table? And how can the table itself, the dialogical seminar table, be reintroduced into an electronically diffuse classroom? How can these socio-technical environments be made more equitable, inclusive, balanced and welcoming for the multiple diversities that they already embody?

DESI Training Centre

Studio Anna Heringer, Rudrapur, Bangladesh, 2008, area: 300 m²

How does this school reorganise the distribution of knowledge and energy?
The construction of the school was intimately linked to the simultaneous organisation of a community, its resources and its needs. It is therefore more accurate to speak of "production" than of construction or architectural design. The building is literally rooted in the soil of the site, with locally sourced rammed earth for its load-bearing walls and lightweight bamboo structures for the upper floors. The construction process was determined by the local workforce and its specific craft.

DESI (Dipshikha Electrical Skill Improvement) is a vocational training centre for electricians. Solar panels power a water pump, which not only allows the building to work properly, but it also acts as a practical laboratory to learn from and to improve. The students are also agents of the replication of this scheme, which they can copy and develop in the territories where they live.

What distinguishes this "classroom" from a conventional learning space?
The climate and, of course, the scarcity of resources, have shaped the school: it is a relatively small building with fluid spaces and thin walls to facilitate natural ventilation. With very limited use of furniture, students and teachers sit on the floor; this allows for more organic groupings, and can thus accommodate different kinds of scenarios or group dynamics. In terms of scale, there is an almost domestic dimension to the way the school is laid out. That is, it is organised into small volumes, assembled together, like the architectural equivalent of a large house or a small village. The classroom (in itself an atypical example, a kind of prototype) is both an enclosed shelter and a stage of possibilities; ultimately, it is a source of knowledge.

Site plan, cross-section and ground floor
Photos © Naquib Hossain, Studio Anna Heringer, B. K. S. Inan

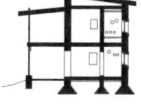

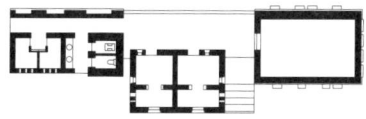

Heinrich-Nordhoff School

Die Baupiloten, Wolfsburg, Germany, 2011–14, area: 1,470 m², number of students: 200

How can all stakeholders be included in the production of an educational environment? The idea of a "quiet, giant meadow" comes from a collage made by a student, Rebecca Schrader. It reflected the wish of the "building family" (students, parents, teachers and building owners) to have a central space, between the classrooms, as a lobby and a place of learning: "On this meadow, one should feel comfortable and be able to exchange ideas". The tall grass creates a sense of security, while a specially designed negotiation game allowed the collective to determine the general configuration of this large space. Several further consultations, informed by more collages and models, then helped to refine the design ideas. That's how the atrium was transformed from a gloomy space into a "quiet, giant meadow".

What distinguishes this "classroom" from a conventional learning space? The renovation of the interior spaces, with custom-made furniture, means they can now be adapted to suit different types of pedagogy; this 1970s building has been revitalised into a welcoming educational space with different areas. The central area, which we call the "marketplace", provides space for different types of learning, assembling and relaxing, while on the opposite side a small stage is provided for lectures or screenings. The modular partitions have several functions and can be used, for example, to pin up ideas and suggestions in the group work area. A third area, for individual study or chilling out, is defined by its beanbags and low tables. The overhanging gallery bridge is used as a homework area. The seating blocks are arranged to allow observation of any experiments being carried out in the science labs.

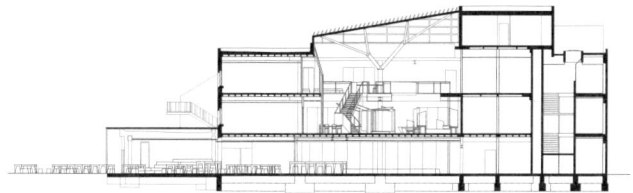

Caneças High School

ARX Portugal Arquitectos, Caneças, Portugal, 2009–13, area: 11,600 m²

How can interaction and informal relationships be encouraged in a school?
The proposal we made for this school is based on a dual interpretation of the notion of learning: that is, both formal and informal learning. In the building, these two categories are reflected in two different architectures, which respond to each other. The rigidity of the existing pavilions, which house the classrooms in a structure made up of authentic "learning machines", thus contrasts with the "informal" character of the new extension, which links together pavilions and floors that were previously isolated from each other. It also creates new collective spaces for "informal learning".

What distinguishes this "classroom" from a conventional learning space?
The belief that all spaces in a school are in fact learning spaces, that each has its role to play, that all are important, and that their organisation and articulation within the school should be fluid, with a high degree of visual and physical permeability. This way, they encourage spontaneous appropriation, and trigger the creative will to learn from (and in) that space. Ultimately, human activities and interpersonal relationships are what form the basis of all knowledge.

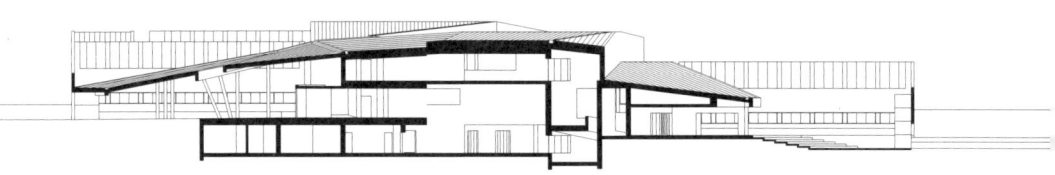

0 | 5 | 10

Garcia de Orta High School

Bak Gordon Arquitectos, Porto, Portugal, 2009–13, area: 10,553 m²

Is it possible to design a building that is a unit but that also allows for future transformations?

At the origin of Parque Escolar (the plan for the modernisation of national secondary education in Portugal), it became apparent that about 75% of Portuguese high schools were laid out in pavilions, based on a rather summary design model, both in terms of future growth and transformation. The system of connections and informal spaces emerged as a possible answer: it allows the scattered pavilions to be read as a single entity, enriched with new spatial and functional valences. Another (perhaps more prosaic) response was to satisfy the need for a collective outdoor covered space. This way, breaktimes could be enjoyed throughout the year, in a city where rain and cold can be a problem for much of the school year.

What distinguishes this "classroom" from a conventional learning space?

The new informal spaces, both indoors and outdoors, allow for less rigid meeting and learning environments, which are different from the traditional classroom model (in which students are placed in front of the teacher). The diversity of pedagogies is thus encouraged, and the whole school community is invited to join these new places. The informal dimension also encourages new forms of responsibility and assertion, both individually and in terms of a revived collective. Our wish is that the community would appropriate the school's central courtyard or — why not? — that it becomes a place for student movements in the fight for a better future. Of course, the memory of the "great span" of Lina Bo Bardi's São Paulo Museum of Art (MASP), the epicentre of so many protests and revolutions, remains very present in our memories.

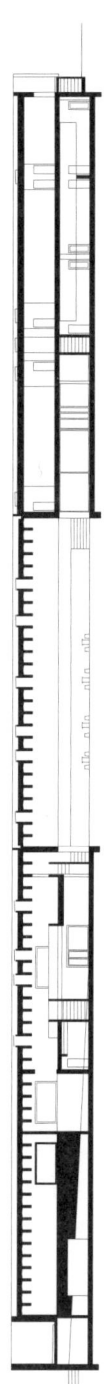

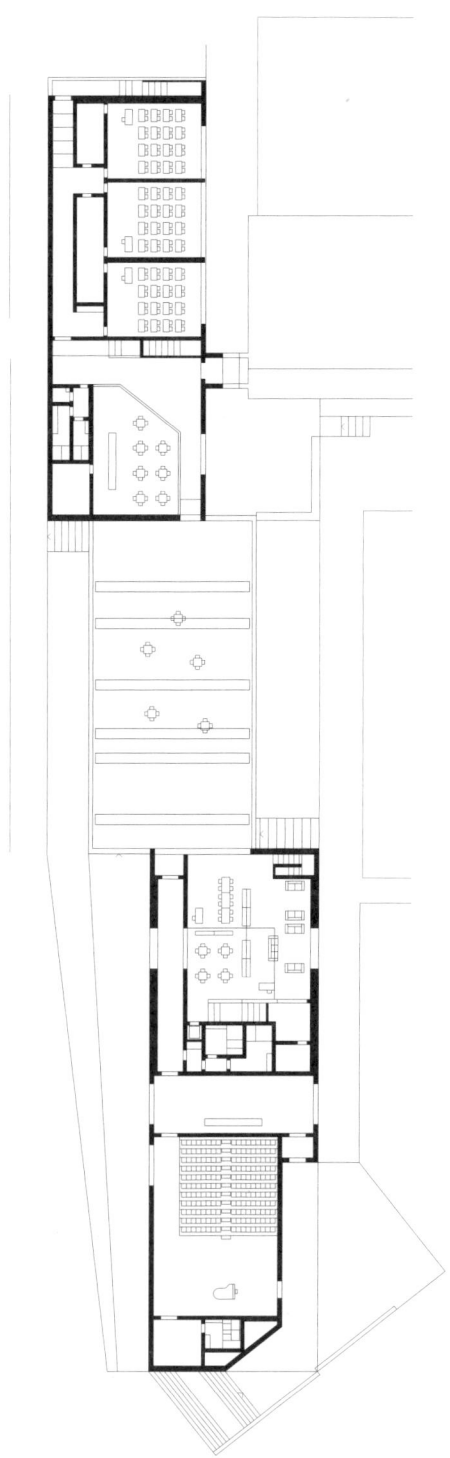

0| |1 |5

Embodiment

This school was built and designed by an architect. I don't remember their name, but this building has become a "historic building", so it's not allowed to be modified or have materials modified, etc.

Adolescence can be described as the movement via which an organism is organised, both in the sense of a process of growth and in the sense that an organism is placed and assigned a role within a wider human collective; the school can be seen as the ecosystem that frames this transition. Roland Bechmann's agricultural high school in Avignon is emblematic of these two scales of growth: the body of the adolescent who is welcomed, nourished, and educated to grow into an adult, and a group called upon to constitute a productive body at the service of industrialised societies.

I think it's changed because it wasn't the same education at that time. Even the education itself has evolved, so the high school followed the development.

ut that's the same, it's evolved over time. Before, it went from father to son, and so on. Now we are specialising in certain points. The high school
cuses on biology and ecology. And we have a very large kitchen department, and we know, more or less, where our products come from. It's all
cal, and they've even managed to adapt the classrooms, for example, which used to be like this one, I imagine. They've managed to adapt them
to a lab, for those studying towards the advanced technician certificate [the BTS].

Lycée Agricole François-Pétrarque

Roland Bechmann
Avignon, France, 1964-68

The farm wasn't the same; they knew how to
adapt it to our needs and to their own needs.

This agricultural school is a milestone project in terms of farming
education. Previously, such a school would have reproduced the
peasantry, but this project transformed the space into a learning
community for farmers, where they could cultivate the soil while going
into higher education. To plant this new seed, one of simultaneous
sowing and learning, several elements had to be added to the cultivated
land: there was an auditorium (linked to a reading garden and library),
a gymnasium with playing fields, and also residential blocks for the
creation of a learning community —a family away from the family.
At the heart of it all was a kitchen and dining room, to share the fruits
of learning.
   The architect Roland Bechmann, along with his collaborator François
Girard, arranged the parts of the new agricultural school into a spiral,
to shelter it from the strong wind of Provence (the Mistral). They
protected each classroom with a patio, where trees could be planted
and rainwater collected. Half a century later, these patios are now
classrooms under the shade of trees, each with its own specific biodiversity; the outdoor classrooms, whether in the open field or the
greenhouses, are now ecological laboratories. The school shares food
with the community and the chef lives in a rooftop apartment of the
central building.

It's the local market for fruit and vegetables and the local farms. We have our own growing
operation too. We sometimes see the cooks walking around the school to collect the spices,
thyme, rosemary etc....

s their choice, but it suits us. We often have
veral choices so it's good. It varies too, all
e time. We like it, so we don't really need to
k what we want.

79

s, a big positive about the school is the canteen.

I'm here because there's rugby. I play rugby in a club in the region, and here it's like a sports centre that specialises in rugby. We have frequent training sessions during the week, and that's why I chose to come to the boarding school, otherwise it was impossible to go back and forth from my home to here, the schedules were too hard... so there you go.

I've also been at the boarding school for two years, I live an hour or so from here, so I chose the boarding school so I wouldn't have to travel. I play rugby at the academy and we do sports practically every day. We get on well together and have a lot of fun.

brings people much closer together. We live together all year round, we spend more time at hool than at home, and we're also from the countryside so we've also learned to live in the y, in contrast.

We learn to live with other students, thanks to the boarding school. We also learn to live in common, because we're often together.

The school, its location, is isolated from the centre of Avignon, so we learn to take public transport. There's more distance to cover in the countryside, you have to go by car.

There are 250 students, and 150 or 200 students studying for the BTS, so that makes a small group of us. Half of us are at the boarding school, so we see each other every morning, every day, every evening. So, it's very much like a family, compared to other schools where there are 1,000 students, where many people don't even know each other, and some of them barely know the teachers. It's like a family here, everybody knows each other, everybody says hello.

In this school there is a "Sentinel" project. "Sentinel" is designed to help other students feel better when they have problems, either at home, or with other students. And this project was set up with the students, with Mrs Garcia who is our dean, with Mathis too, and also with the teachers. I participate in school life by being part of this project.

e teachers, the management, the school administration office here: ey are very attentive to the students, they propose projects, things e that; for example, we are with you at the moment. And we partici- te a lot in the school's opinions, and in what we can offer to the hool too.

81

r example, last week, there were inspectors: they asked us what needs to be improved at the school, they asked about the od aspects, the not-so-good, what we would like to add.

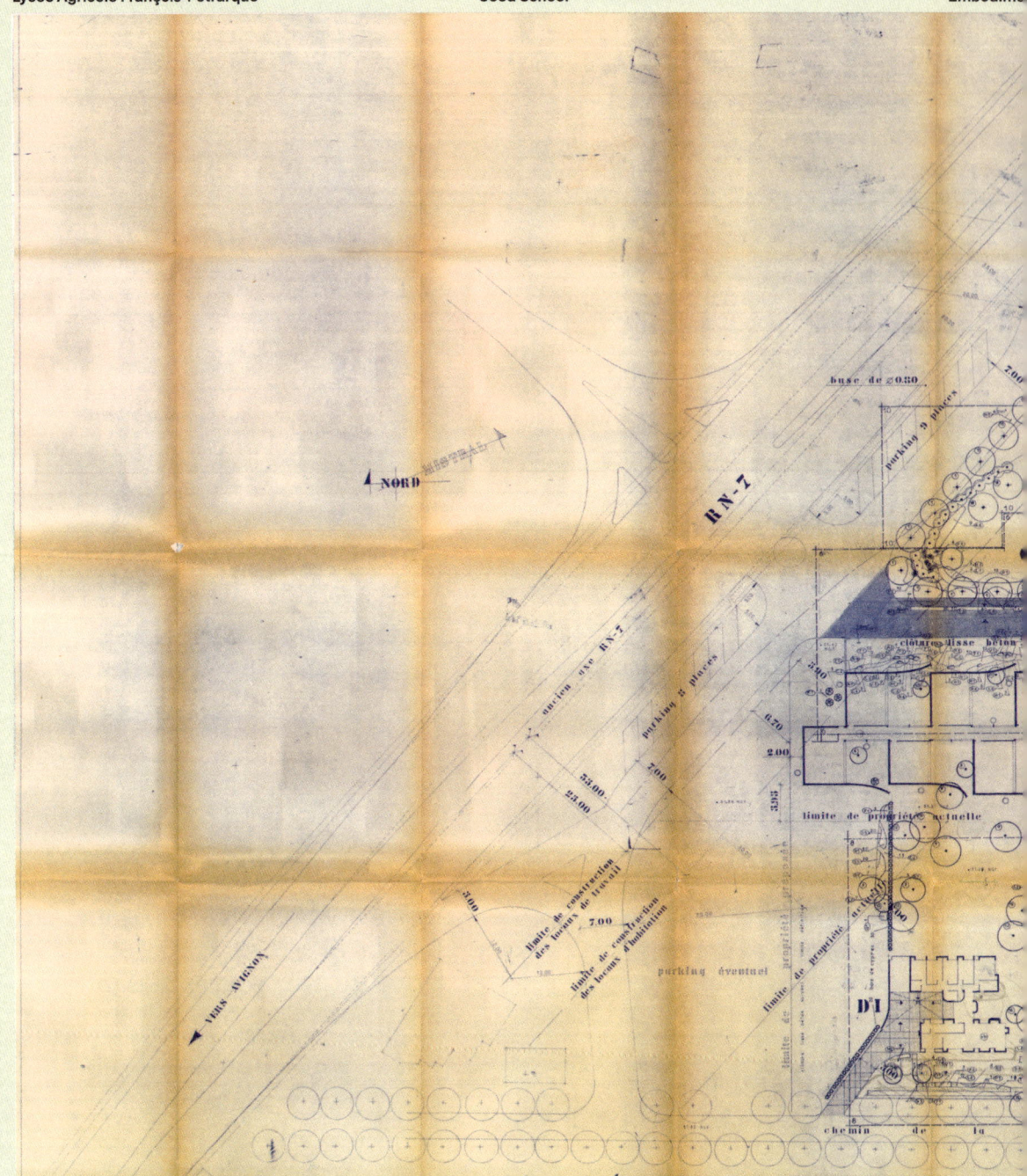

© Archives of the Cité de l'Architecture et du Patrimoine, Paris

In this building there's a teaching kitchen. This is where we, the final
year students, do our farming machinery.

So now we're coming to the high school farm, we'll start with the BTS and final-year classes, and then we'll go and see
the greenhouses.

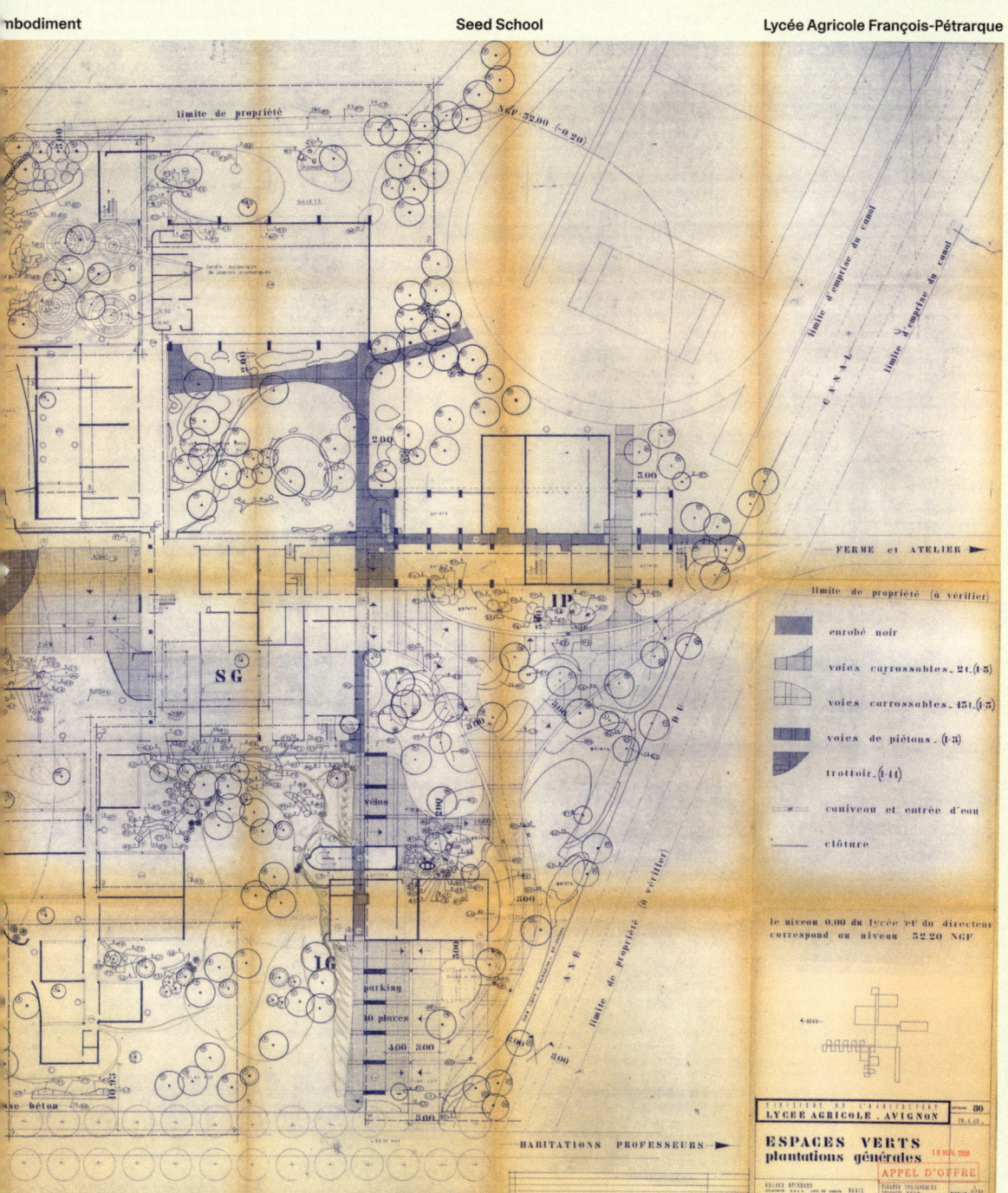

ere's a lot of work behind the farm, there's hectares, it's a hundred metres or more. It's quite
ce to walk around, if there's only two or three of us just to visit. I will show you what we grow.

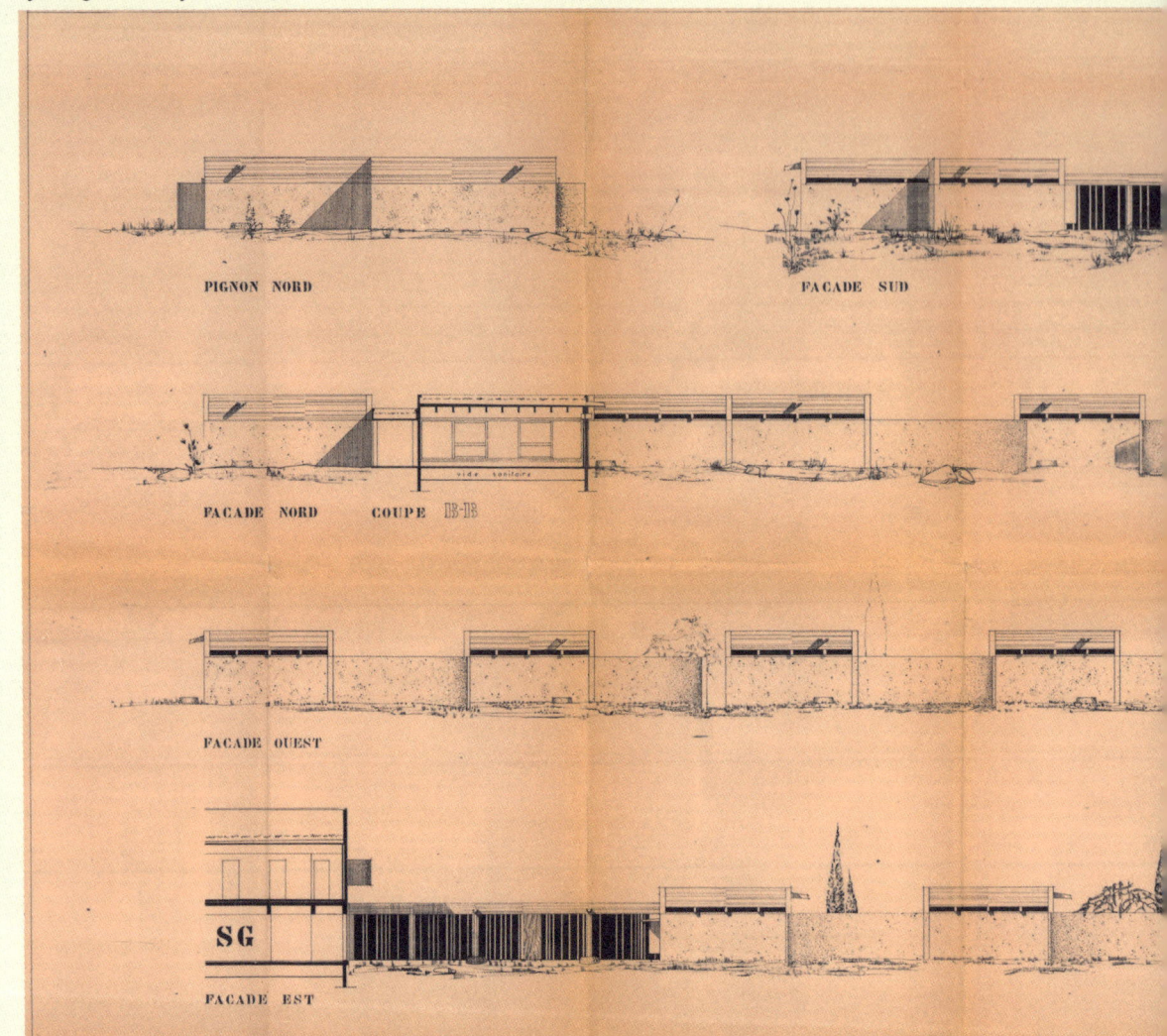

PIGNON NORD

FACADE SUD

FACADE NORD   COUPE B-B

FACADE OUEST

SG

FACADE EST

Then we'll go to the farm and see the different types of crops we have.

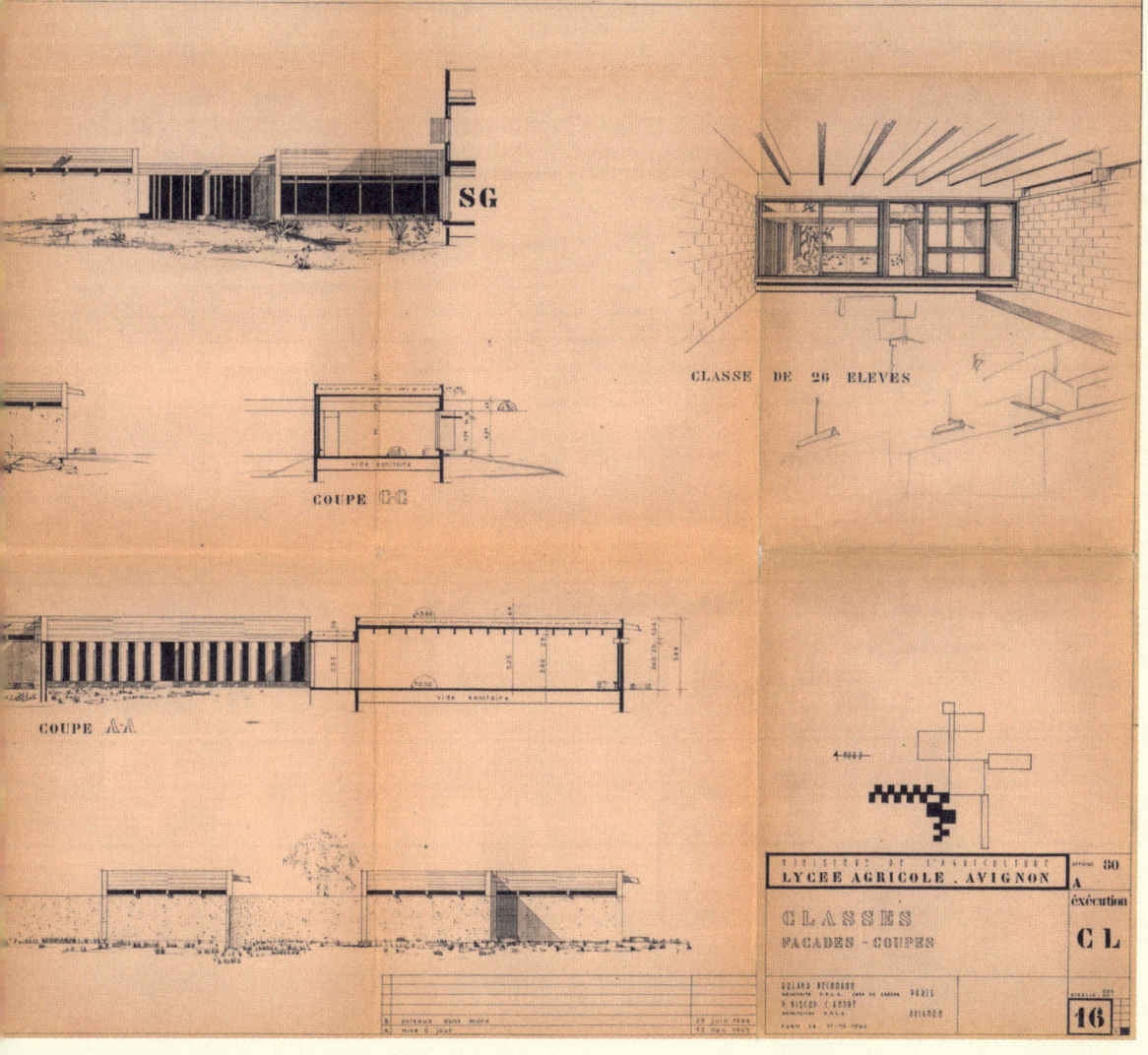

nd the BTS students work here, they are here most of the time during
e day, they have all their courses here, they have the teaching
tchen which is here.

e're arriving at the classroom. There we have the teaching kitchen, then the BTS and classrooms, and here we do agro-equipment.
e BTS do everything about agronomy, and French I think, farming machinery if they have it too. Well, it's quite broad.
ter the final year, they also do courses here, so we don't have much farming machinery. There's everything you need here for the
nal-year course.

And the shed where we have the farm equipment, all the tractors, the brush cutters.

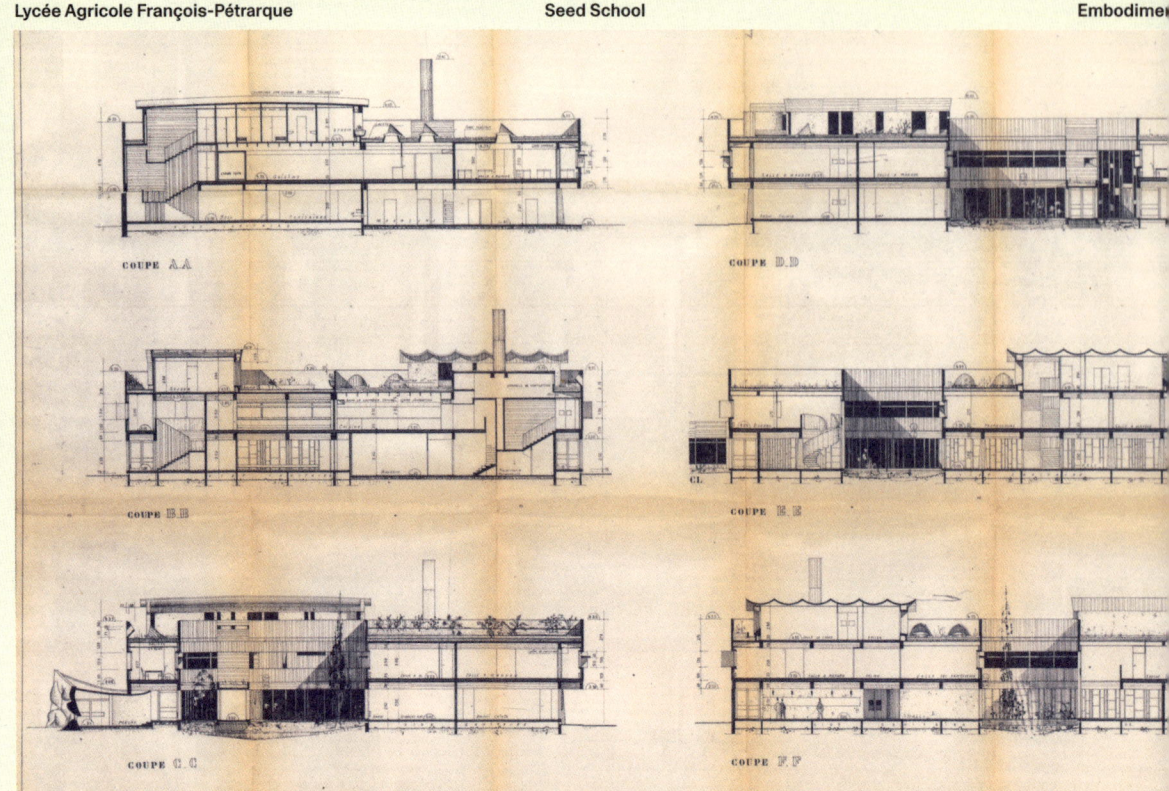

Sometimes we do little experiments on the farm, things like that, but it doesn't really prepare us for future work. The problem is that they don't teach us how to make a CV, how to apply for a job — they might just teach us group cohesion, work motivation, autonomy...

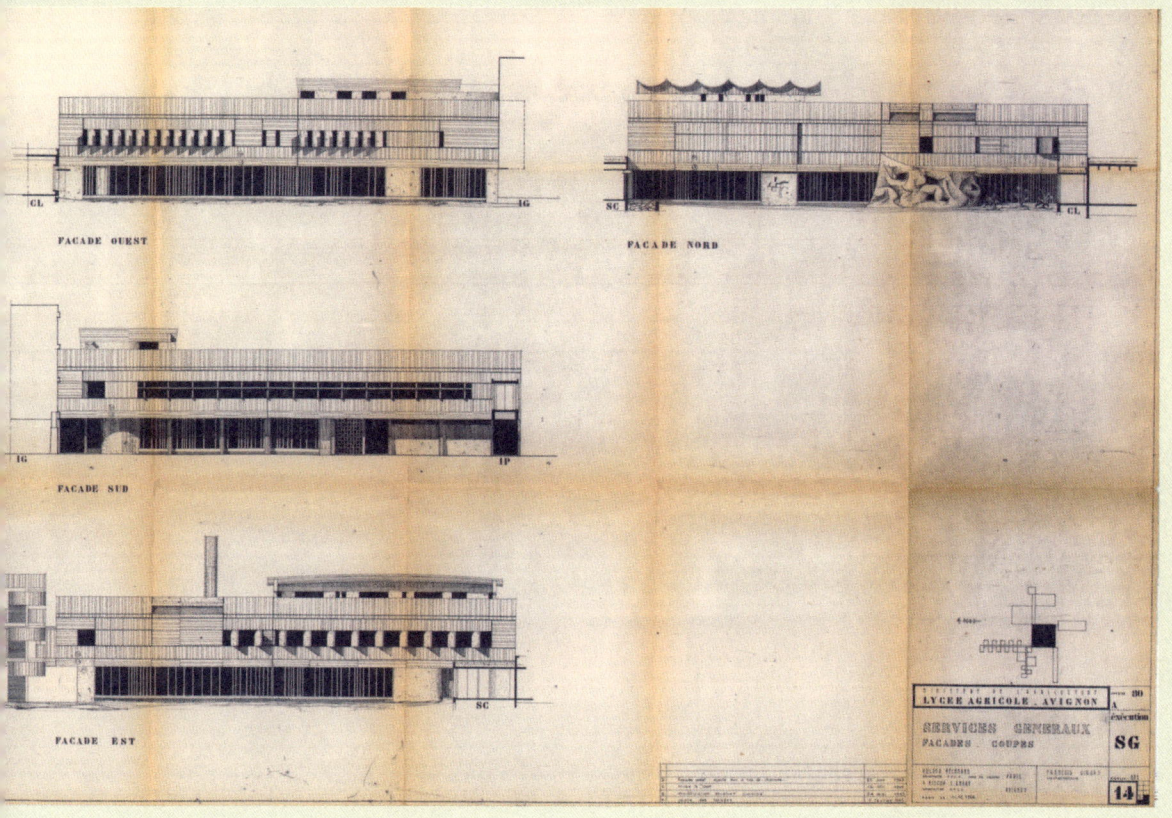

o, here we are in the greenhouse, we grow
everal crops. Here there are courgettes, they
re organic: we don't use any fertilisers or
esticides. And we often eat the foods we
row in the canteen, where they are cooked by
e chef.

the greenhouse there are several varieties all year round: we change them a lot, the culture is very diverse, so we get
rough a lot of products.

Here there are orchards that are based on agroforestry, which is a dynamic system of natural
resource management that reduces inputs, develops cultivated biodiversity, and improves soil
productivity.

The advantage is also that with our STAV Bac [Baccalaureate in Science and Technologies of Agronomy and Living Organisms] we have an internship to do, five weeks on a farm, and that integrates us into the working world.

I think that the teachers are quite caring about our future, we often do "life classes" to know where we want to go. Yes, that's it, to update our ideas, our thoughts, and what we would like to do later.

Then they help us with the procedures.

Yes, for example, for the internship, they helped us a lot with the procedures. For some, even if it was far away from the school, they went to the internship to see if it was going well. In fact, they are very involved in what they do at school with the students.

"Direct sale" is when the products grown and produced here are sold directly on the farm. The food is mostly used for the canteen, for the students, but we also sell some of it, we sell strawberries, we sell peaches... We turn the grapes into grape juice.

Embodied Energy and Nourishment: Laboratory and Nursery

Paying greater attention to ecology, food production, circular economy, as well as a systemic understanding of classrooms as an intertwined network, will increase the resilience and the overall awareness of the energy footprint of learning architectures. This would be aided by shortening farm-to-table food cycles or edible schoolyard-to-lunchroom table cycles, improving diets, decreasing food waste and water consumption, and cutting greenhouse gas emissions. The use of renewable materials like wood, the collection and deployment of rainwater, or ecological sewage treatment systems, are just some of the ways in which educational environments can be object lessons in the making of a present that does not compromise the future.

De Wijnpers Agricultural School

OFFICE Kersten Geers David Van Severen, Leuven, Belgium, 2011–15, area: 4,000 m²

What does a classroom look like in an agricultural high school?

In an agricultural high school, a large part of the learning takes place outdoors, in direct contact with the natural elements. So, the question that arises is "where is the classroom?". The main educational space, which has no walls or ceiling, is simply the ground, or rather the soil, on which students experiment and learn to grow food plants. In the last phase of their growth, nutrition and physical education play a special role in building their bodies, both physically and socially, as these young people enter adulthood.

What distinguishes this "classroom" from a conventional learning space?

This school is built in the transitional space between two levels and two different types of land (for sports and farming), so it acts as a kind of "inhabited wall" that connects these spaces instead of separating them. Although working with the land, hands on, is a fundamental part of this education, it is also essential to have the space and distance to reflect, monitor and test, in order to gain the experience needed to turn what would otherwise be a mere manual skill into a profession. The six-storey building, rising above the plantations, offers precisely these resources: there are laboratories, an auditorium and even classic classrooms overlooking the surroundings.

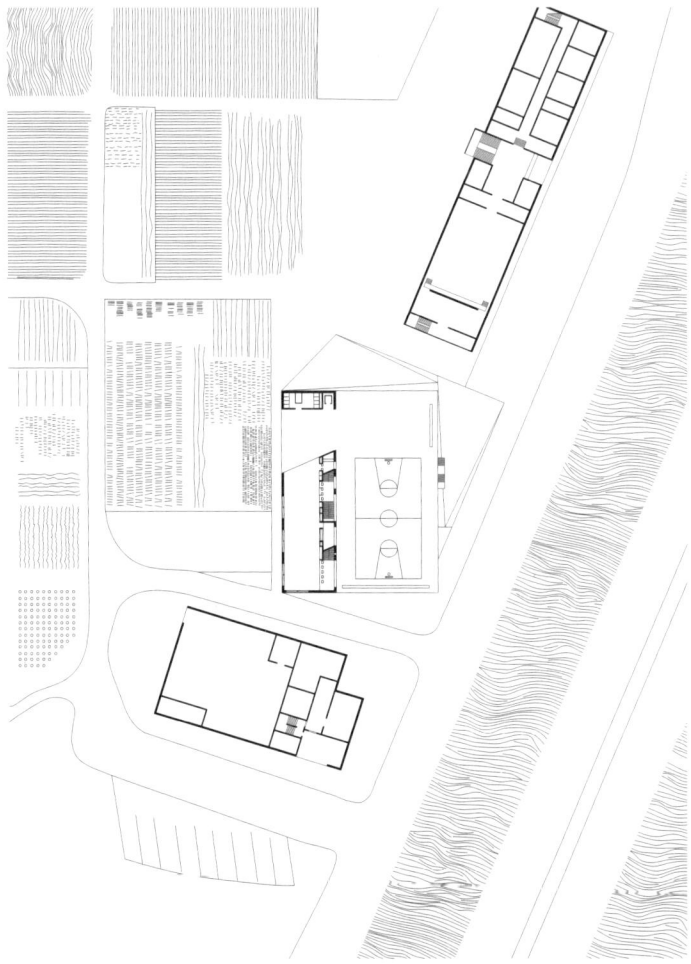

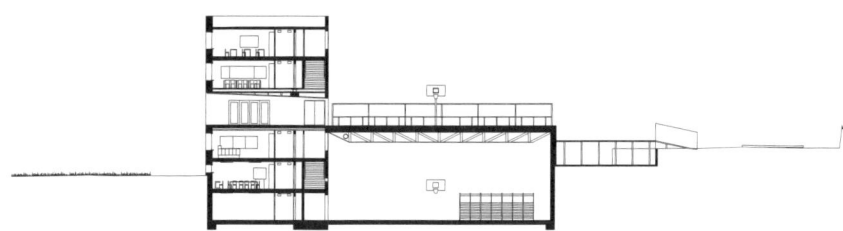

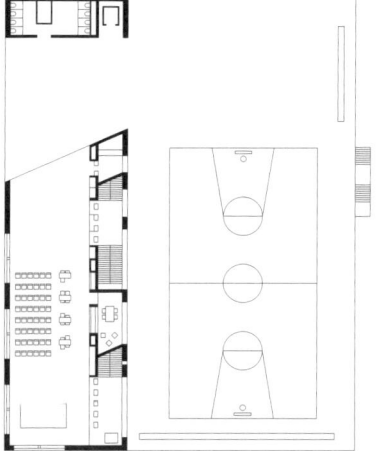

Schmuttertal High School

HK Architekten + Florian Nagler Architekten, Diedorf, Germany, 2015, area: 7,816 m²

How to make classrooms both healthy and ecological?

The transition from childhood to adulthood requires a greater understanding of the world, in order to be able to transform it. With this in mind, the design of the Schmuttertal High School was designed as a research project for the German Federal Foundation for the Environment (DBU). The school is in fact a testing ground for an ambitious proposal, aimed at many students (around 1,000), in a structure that offers a healthy and comfortable environment for these developing bodies, without compromising possible future changes. The building is modular, so that it can be adapted to possible changes in the curriculum. It uses wood as the main building material and produces more energy than it consumes, resulting in a positive carbon and energy balance.

What distinguishes this "classroom" from a conventional learning space?

Most of the classrooms here follow a pattern that could be described as "conventional": they are rectangular rooms, with great attention paid to the treatment of natural light, thermal comfort and ventilation. However, in order to make the building futureproof, one classroom in five is envisaged as a "market place". More than a classroom, this place is thus conceived as a "space of possibilities", equipped with educational material and freely accessible computer workstations that can be used by both students and teachers to try out alternative forms of teaching, teamwork or self-responsible learning methods.

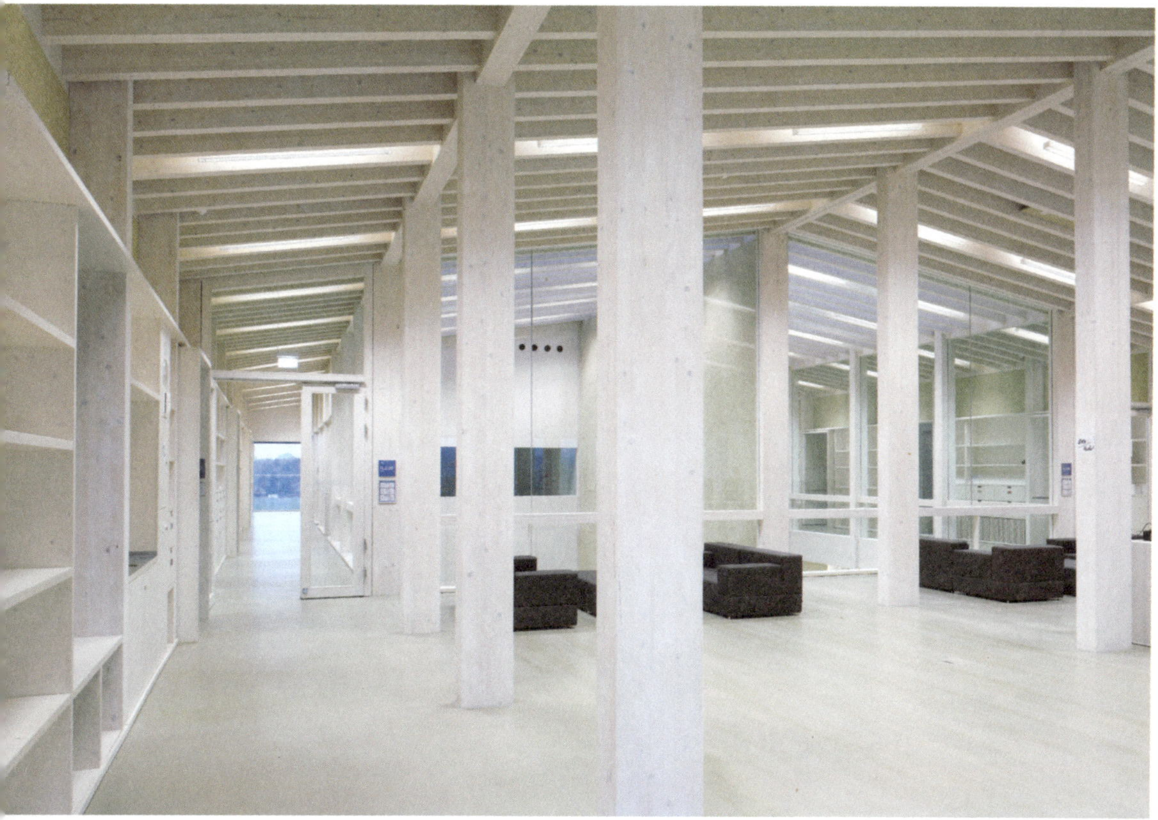

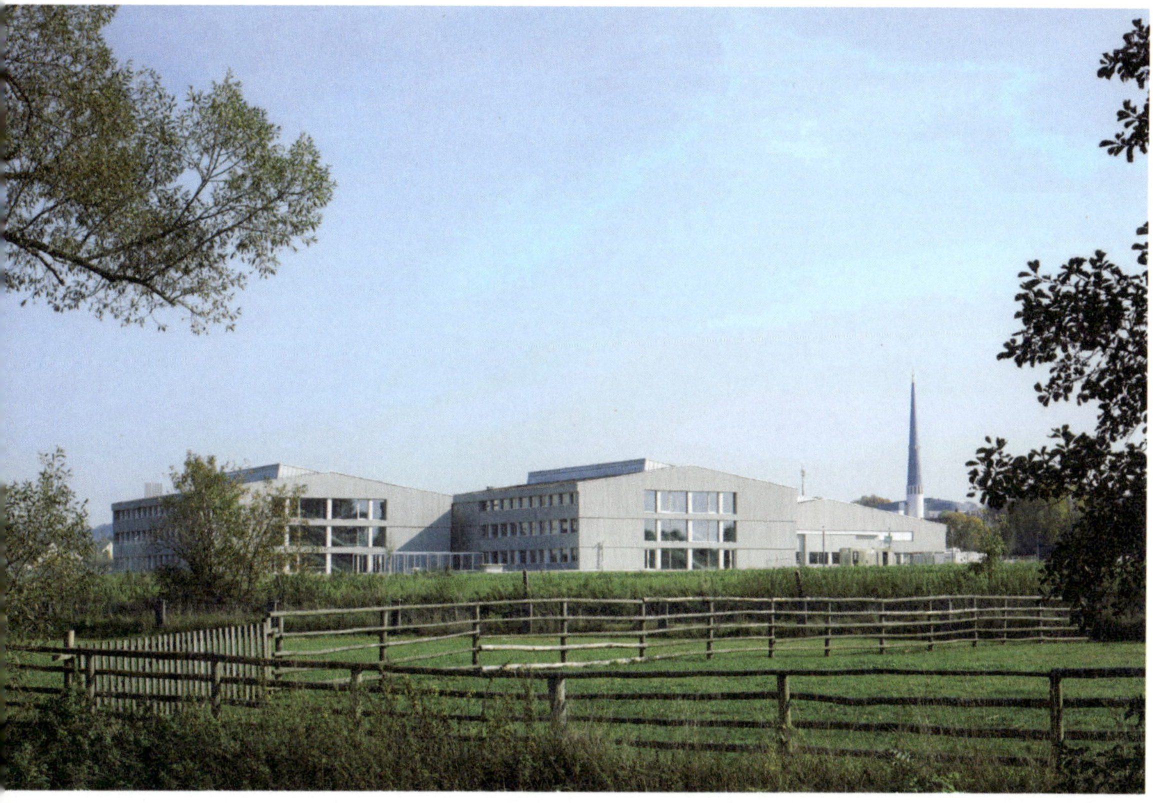

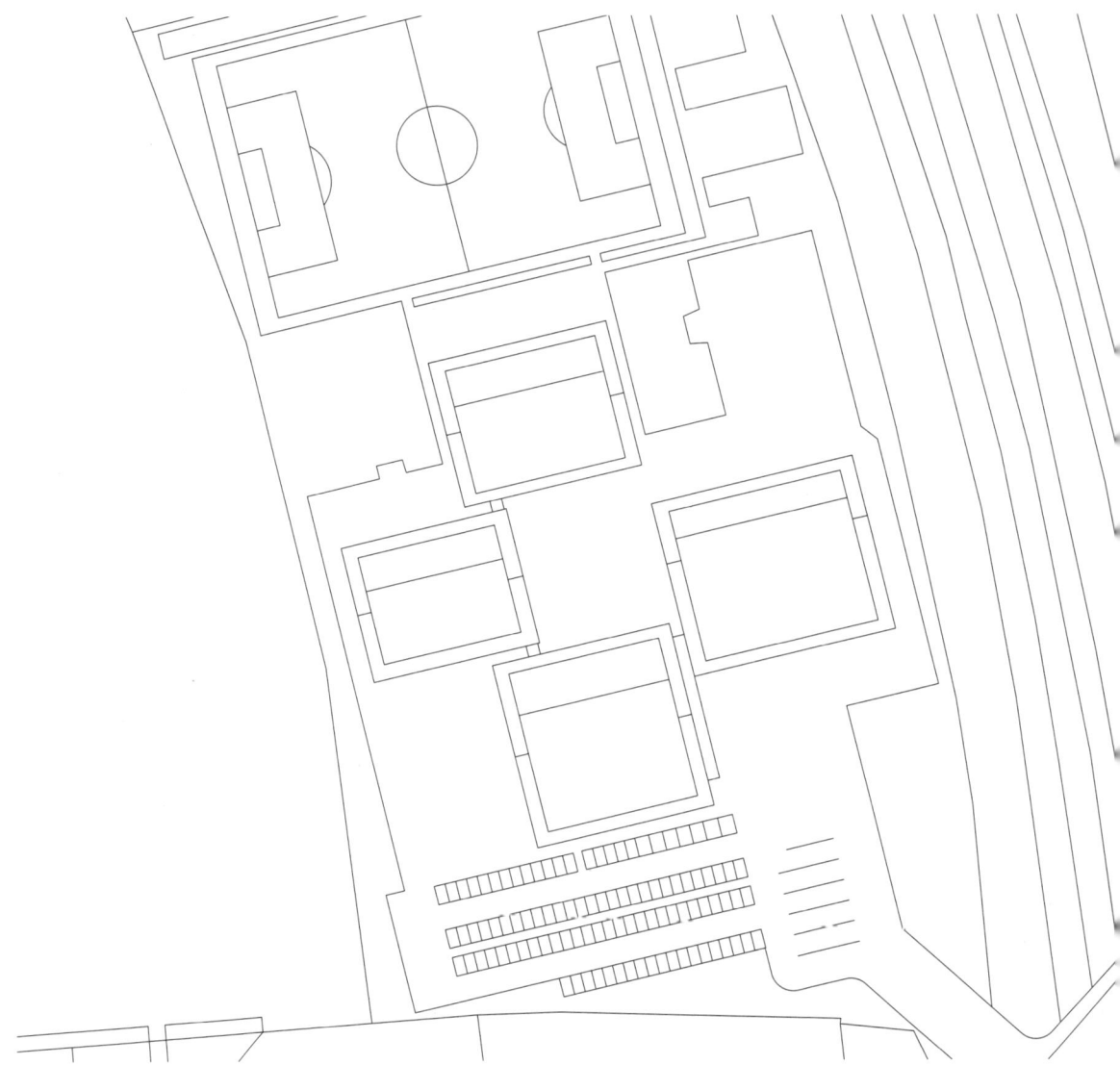

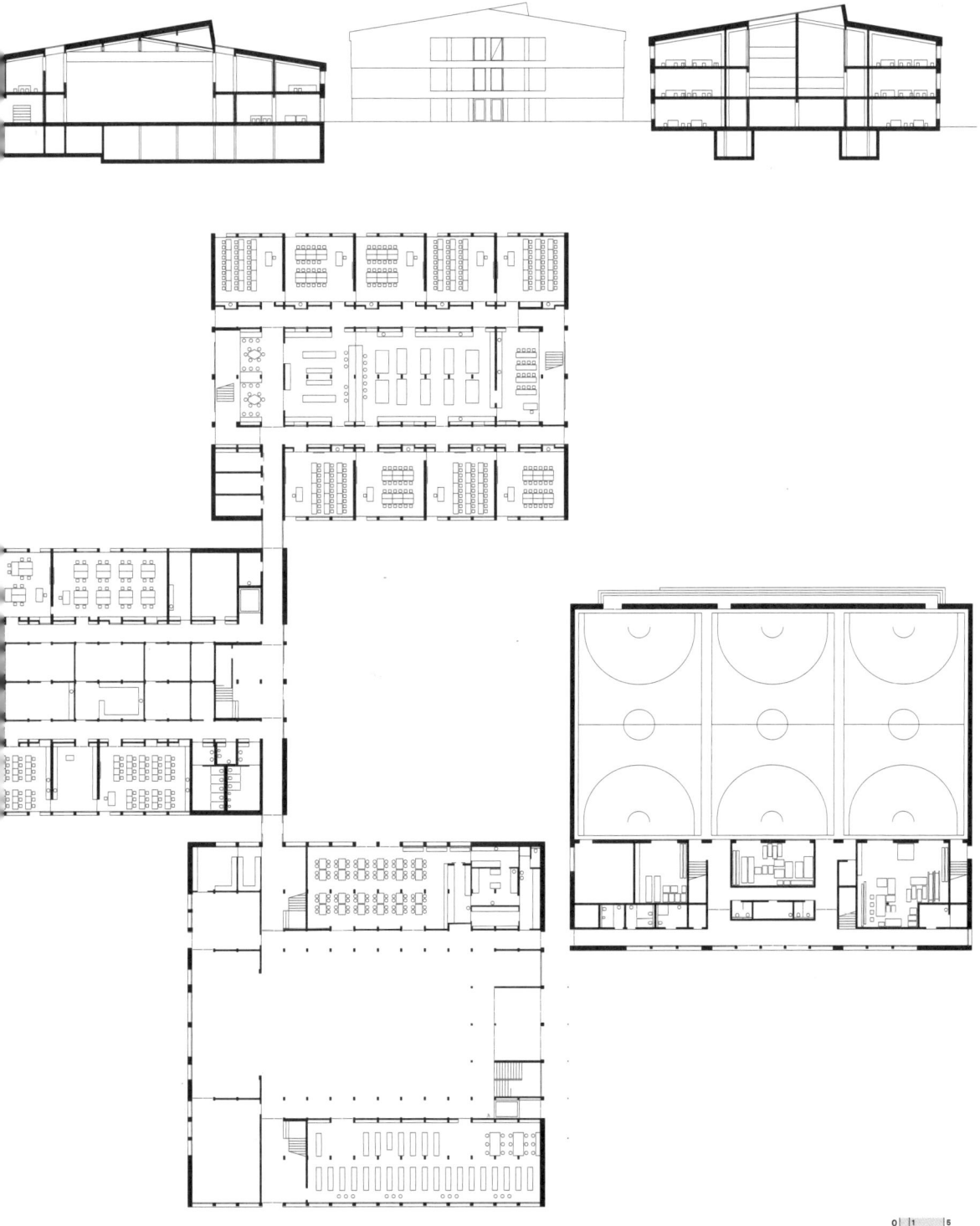

Schorge High School

Kéré Architecture, Koudougou, Burkina Faso, 2016, area: 1,660 m²

How can local resources be mobilised to design a high school?

This school is located in a relatively populated region, but still it is built on a large, flat piece of land, exposed to the sun, hot winds and dust. The building as a whole therefore aims to protect its users from this hostile environment, using locally sourced materials, assembled in such a way as to provide good internal comfort. Laterite — extracted from the surrounding area and easily cut into bricks which are then left to dry in the sun — increases the thermal mass of the main walls. Shading devices, made of steel or eucalyptus trunks, provide additional protection from the sun's rays. Wind shafts on the roof echo meticulously positioned ventilation openings to act as natural coolers.

What distinguishes this "classroom" from a conventional learning space?

The classrooms are designed in a fairly classical way: they are rectangular, and are the only enclosed spaces in the whole building. Like the surrounding houses, they are arranged in a circle around an inner courtyard. The secondary façade, made up of thin trunks placed vertically, gives the whole a homogeneous appearance, while creating a shaded intermediate space. While the central courtyard allows for large outdoor gatherings, the corridor around it offers a shaded area (with benches made from leftover building materials) for smaller group gatherings.

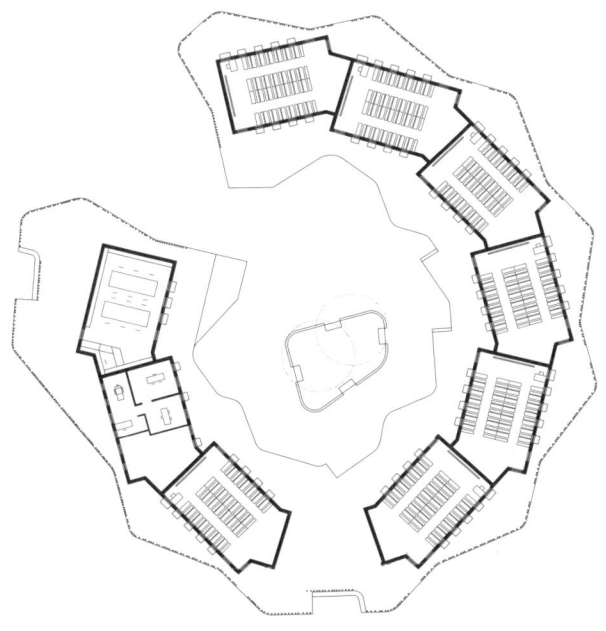

0| |1 |5

© Aurélio Vaz

Assembly

The protesting spirit of the militant teenager, not old enough to vote, is central to the politics of the second half of the 20th century. It is structured by high school revolts which sometimes partake in wider contestations, and sometimes precede or even trigger them. The constitution of adolescence as a political body is carried out via the places where teenagers gather, mainly the street, but also in leisure and learning spaces. The polygonal aula of the Geschwister-Scholl-Gesamtschule in Lünen, completed in 1962 by Hans Scharoun, is one of those utopian spaces that embed a democratic and collective use within the form of a building.

I would like people to be allowed to use certain rooms, for example, the student room, so you could go there during the break if you have a headache or something.

It was kind of hard to listen to one person for six or nine hours, because we couldn't just take out a mobile phone and write an email or something like that. So, we had to go through the entire lesson and listen. And that was hard.

Now you come to school at 8:00 and go home at 16:00 or something. But at home it was like it started at 8:00 and went on until 16:00. But after 16:00 you had so much homework, so much learning to do... Then it was like 20:00 in the evening, and I was like, "Oh, my day is over and tomorrow I need to go to school again!".

It was like your whole life was just school, school. No free time at all! You couldn't go out because of the pandemic, and you couldn't visit your friends. And it was hard. It was very, very hard. And, in my opinion, you can see this today too. It's very hard. So, we have no balance.

© Aurélio Vaz

Geschwister-Scholl
Secondary School
Hans Scharoun
Lünen, Germany, 1964-69

The school belongs to the students because they're the ones using it.

Hans Scharoun's spatial and political reflection on spaces of learning is concretised in Lünen through the central space of the forum, or market. This square arranges collective life and groups together, for the various moments of learning: there is a neighbourhood of quasi-domestic classroom units (with an entrance lobby, a pentagonal central space, a nook for group work and an autonomous outdoor space), a science block (with laboratory spaces and small auditoriums), an arts education area (where sliding doors divide the music space, which faces the playground, and the visual arts, facing the street), and, at the junction with the school's entrance, a parliament (a large polygonal space where the entire learning community can meet face-to-face, in assembly).

Founded as a secondary school for girls, it was an institution of great pedagogical innovation: there were spaces adapted to suit the care of different ages, and a colour scheme to distinguish spaces and guide movement. Today, it can be read as a remarkable example of convergence between space and pedagogy. The school has undergone major transformations in these relationships; its interiors were once fully painted white, because a uniform colour seemed more inclusive than the singularity of stained glass or reflections. But everything changes, things and relationships, and today this school experiences a diversity that goes far beyond gender. It was listed as a modern heritage site, and its philologically restored splendour prepares it again for new encounters and disagreements with the turbulence of adolescence.

think the concept of
e school is a little bit
fferent. I mean, Hans
charoun was
inking about a
arket, so you could walk around and see each
her, like in a market. And the classrooms are
ery different, actually everything is different.
ut, I mean, of course, the lessons and the
ubjects are the same as in other schools.

he school is the same... but the curriculum
anges every year, a little bit.

think the curriculum changed very much because the school was at first a woman's school, a girl's school. Now there
e students from grades 5 to 13, so many people of all ethnicities and of all genders, and I think you have to change the
rriculum a little bit to make it more individual for all students in the school.

© Aurélio Vaz

REC TC: 00

I think the school gets more diverse every year. So, it's just nice to see how many different people you can have here. And I also think that the classrooms were separated, the boys on one side and the girls on the other. The girls probably had different sport lessons to the boys, but I'm not sure.

We eat here, we can also buy snacks like cheese rolls, chocolate buns or things like *Schnitzel* or pasta and eat them, but you need to pay, of course. Or you can go at breaktime and buy some cakes there.

It's from Kanne, a big local bakery. All food comes from there. There is a big Kanne in the city centre. But we can buy their products a little bit cheaper here.

The meat for Muslim students is chicken, not pork. That way, the Muslim students can also eat here, and they're freer to decide what they want to eat. Because Muslims and Jewish people cannot eat every meat.

think you can also order vegetarian dishes. And we can order some egan products like *Laubenstange* bread rolls. So it's really nice. You eed to ask to find out, like "is this vegetarian or not?".

We don't have the same food every day. We have a school shop, there are sandwiches, waffles, drinks too, then we have the lunch station where you can order food for the next day, and there you can have things like *Schnitzel* or soup. So today, for example, I didn't order lunch because I went to get a roll, but I usually order there quite often.

Sometimes it's just friends eating together, or sometimes it's other people eating together, or classmates.

e are the SV [*Schülervertretung*, the student council], so we repre-
ent the students here. If they have a problem, of course, they can go to
eir teacher or something, but they can also come to us and say like,
eah, we don't want this or we want this", and we can organise a
eeting about it.

e are also in direct contact with the school director, and that's why we represent all the
udents in the school. And I think our role is a very important one, because there are children
ho are afraid to speak to the other students. The teacher can come to us and we also try our
est to help them, and we also try to do something and help all the students in the same way.

There are six teachers, six parents and six of us students in the SV, so everybody can have a voice and decide on important things for the school.

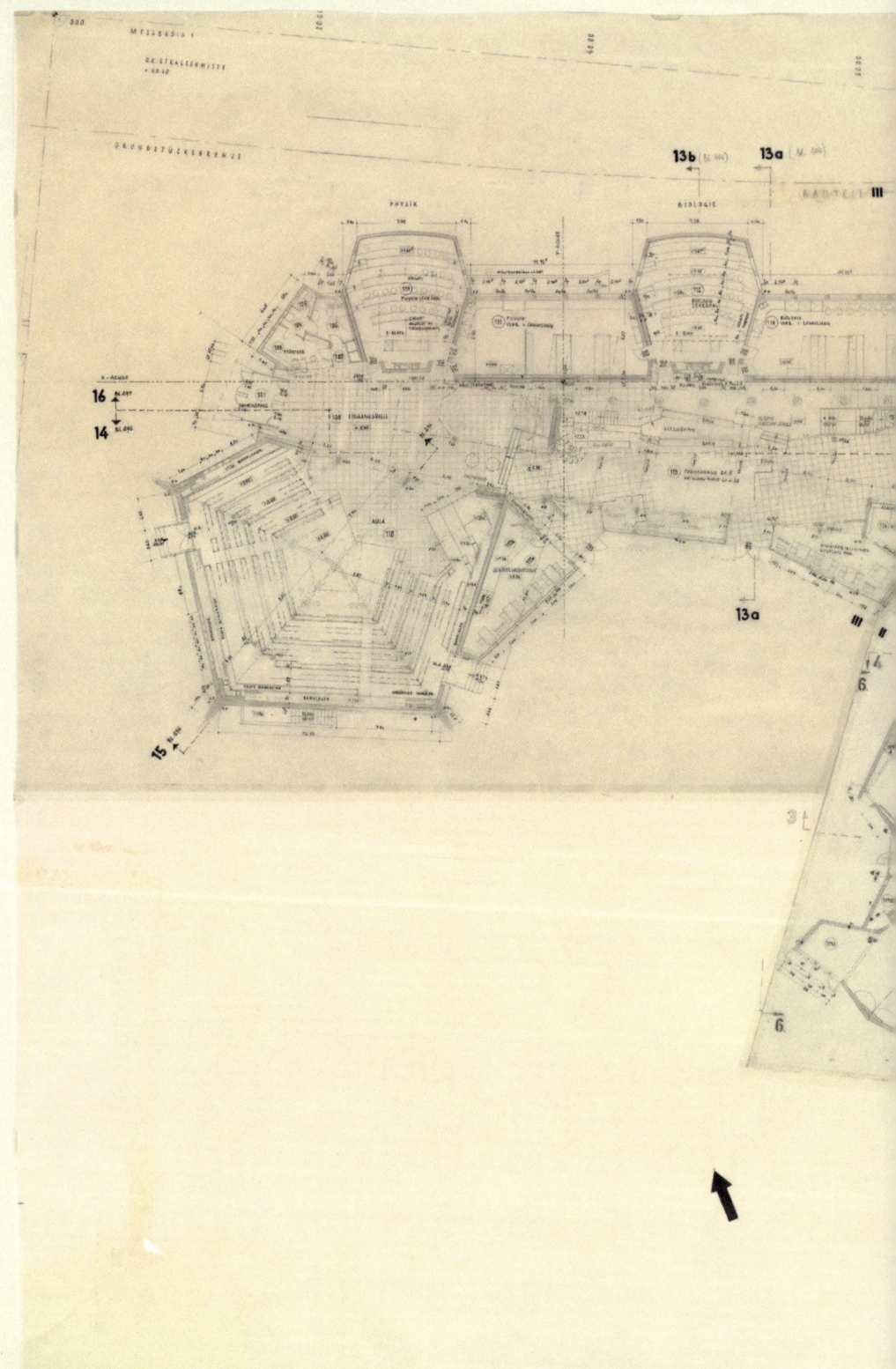

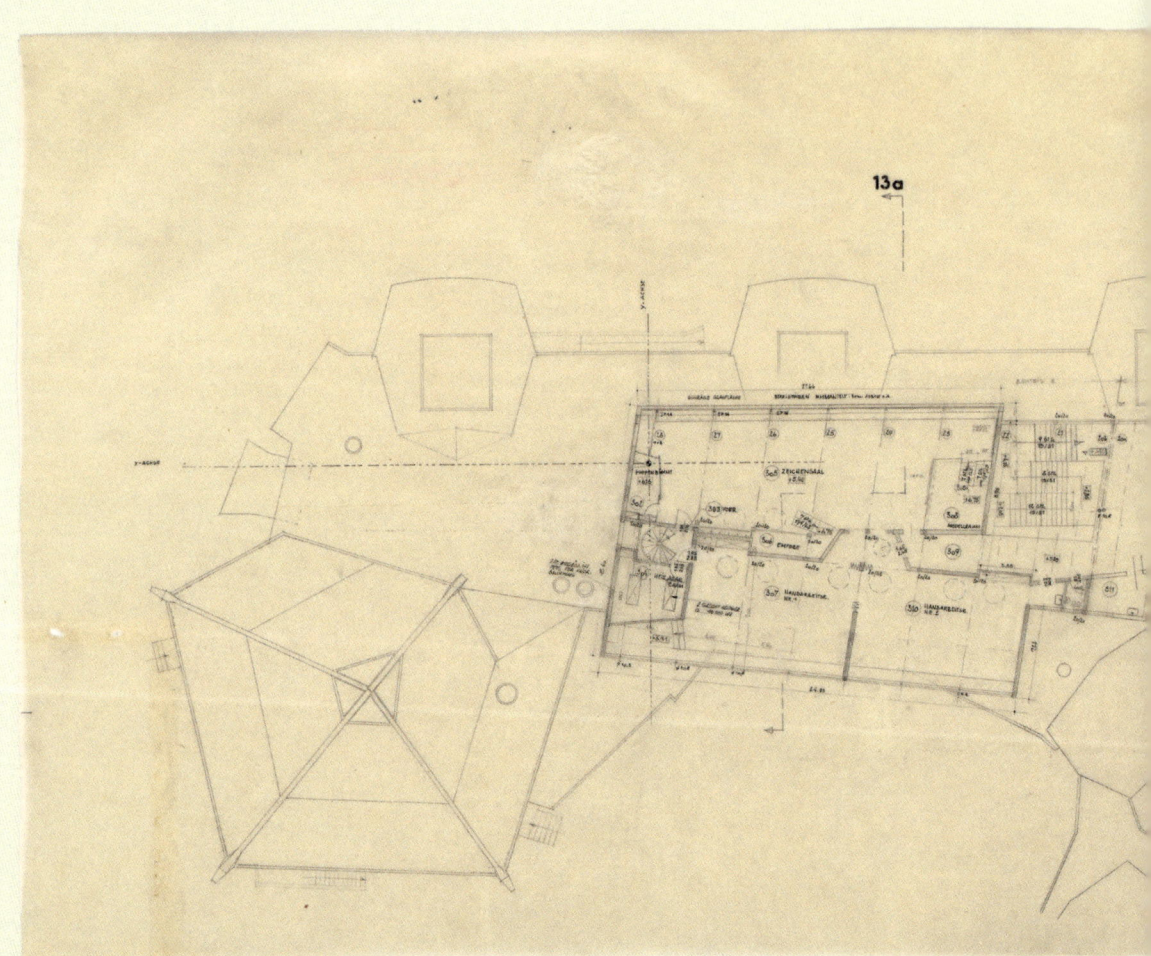

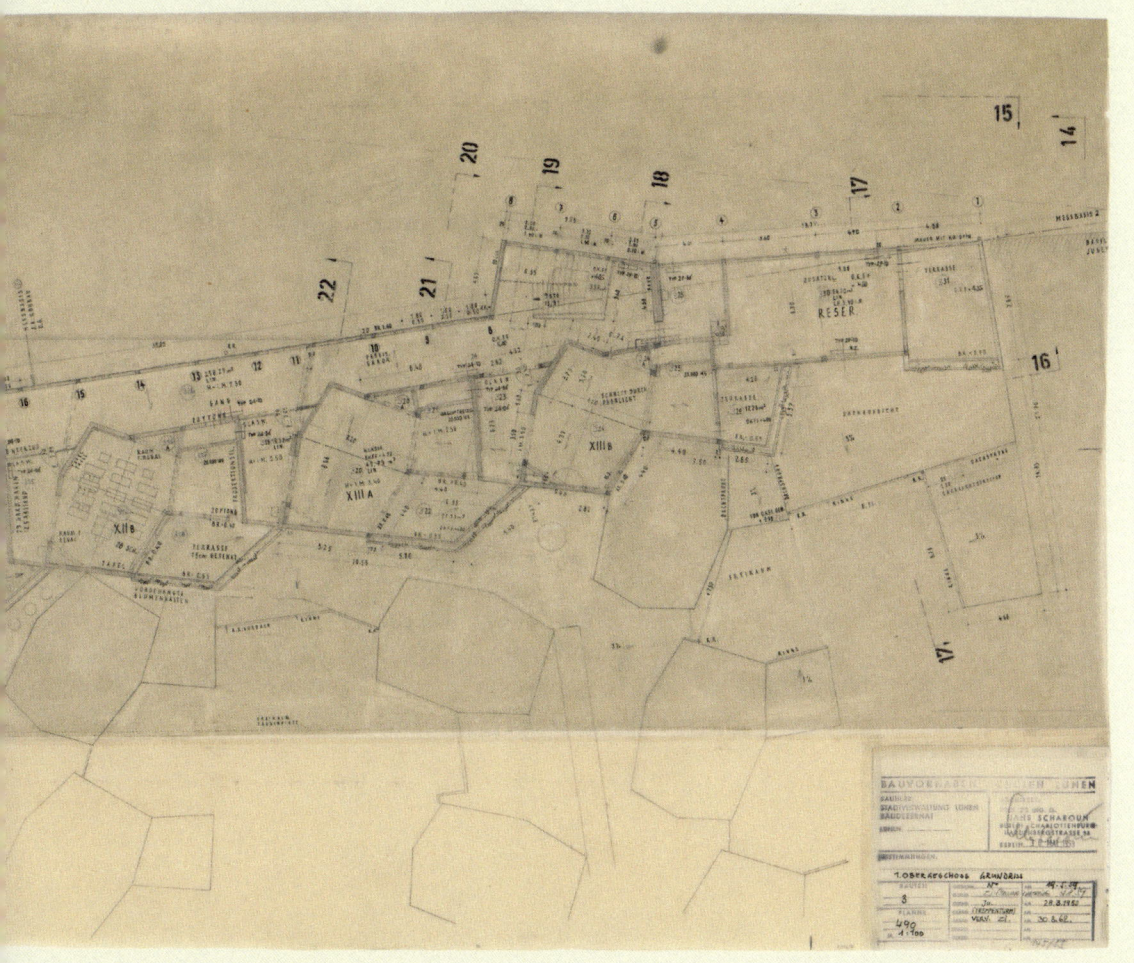

The important conversations happen during breaktime, because you are not in the lesson anymore and you can talk with your friends and that's very important. If I didn't understand something I can ask my friends again, and maybe we will learn during breaks. We talk about other stuff on the breaks and that's very good too.

We also talk about important things during some special moments, like when a teacher is sick and we don't have class. We gather in the cafeteria and eat and talk about the school. If we have homework to do, we do it there and we help each other, or show each other the homework.

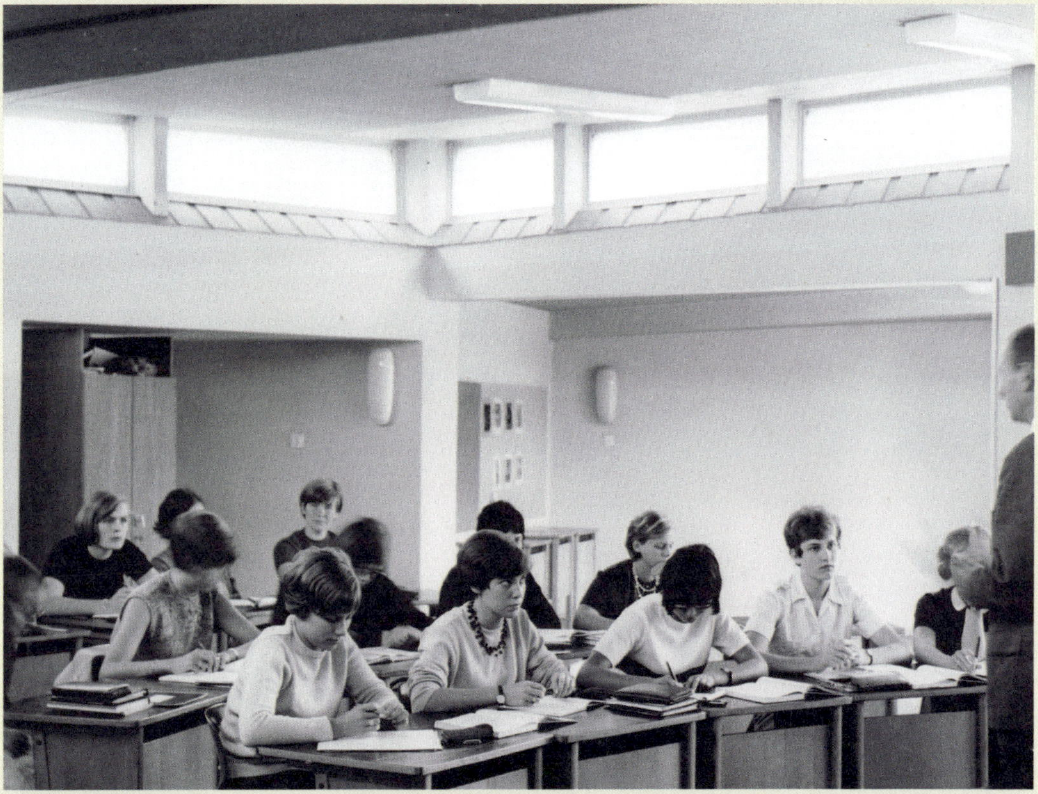

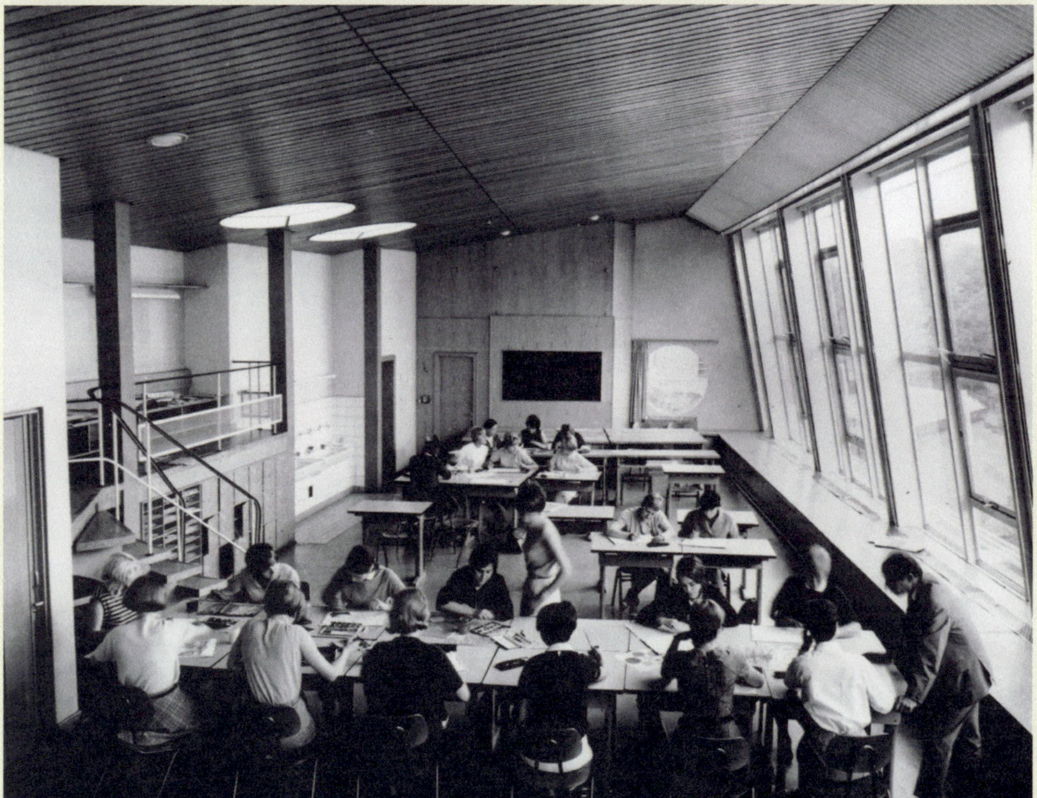

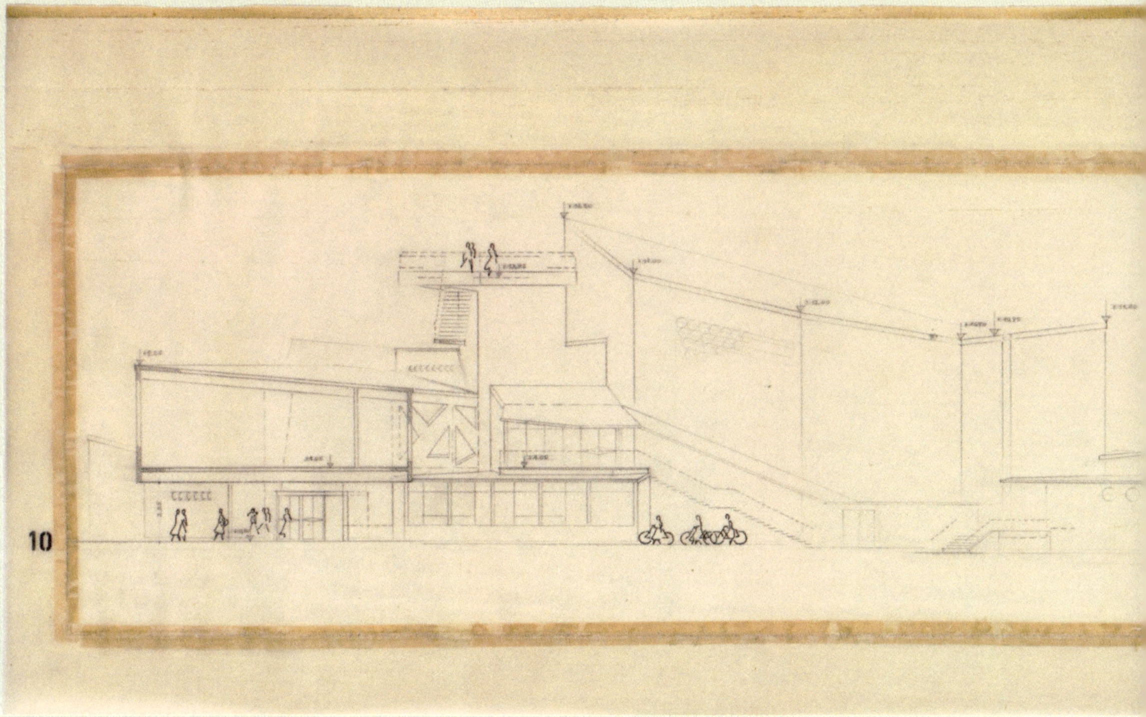

10

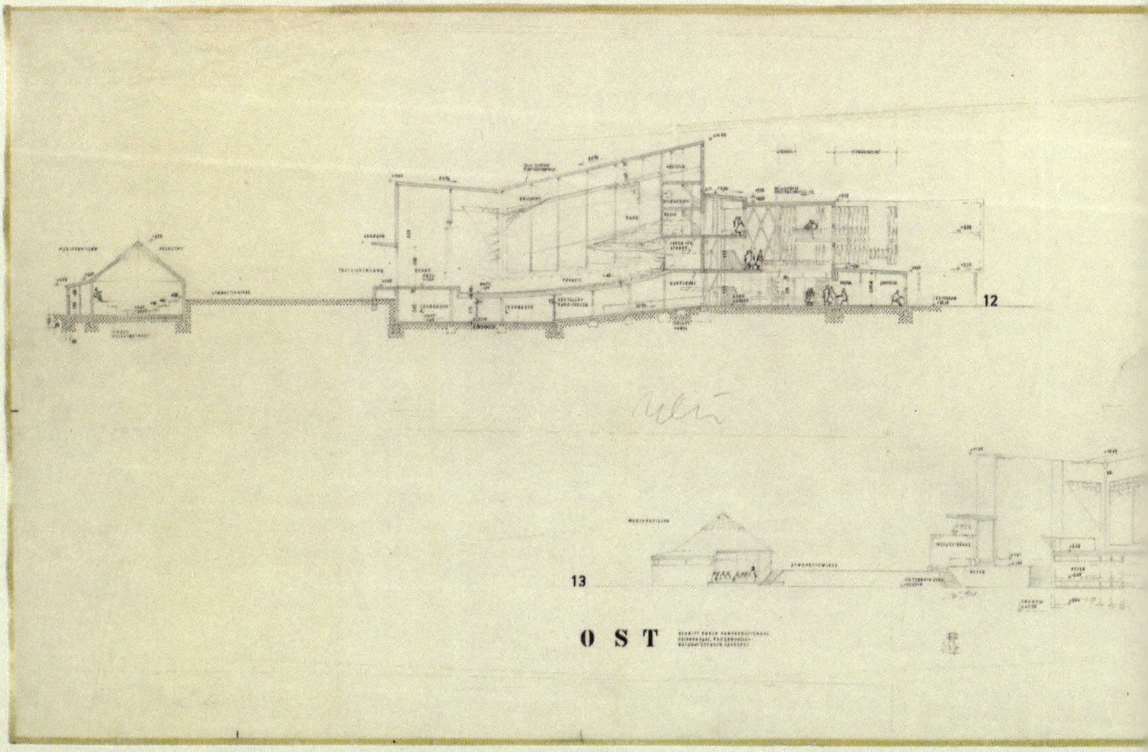

12

13

OST

e already have a lot of options in this school. We have a kitchen, we have drama classes, we have AG
rbeitsgemeinschaften], which are sort of working groups that gather after school, in which you can meet up with other
udents, on a voluntary basis, to discuss certain topics like sport, music or international exchanges.

lso believe that all the students think like this, because we represent our students. We find out if there are problems, and we hear about what
e can do better, and all these things. And if students think that something is bad, I think we should know that.

, if we had to make a wish for our school, we
ouldn't wish for anything: all we can imagine
already here.

                                        Longer breaktimes!

                                        We have different activities, like we have chemistry, physics, sport activities,
                                        biology, baking, cooking... Everything that you can think of.

        I think all the students really like the school because of the many options we
        have. We also have therapists, and if we have problems, we can meet them
        and tell them. And then they try to make our situation better. So I really can't
        imagine that anybody is unhappy here.

Well, it's like this: even if you feel very bad, you can't go in there. But they made it like that because of Corona, so you are not
allowed to be in the hall during breaktime. And I would also change that, so you can be spend your breaks there again.

                                        During the pandemic we learned at home.

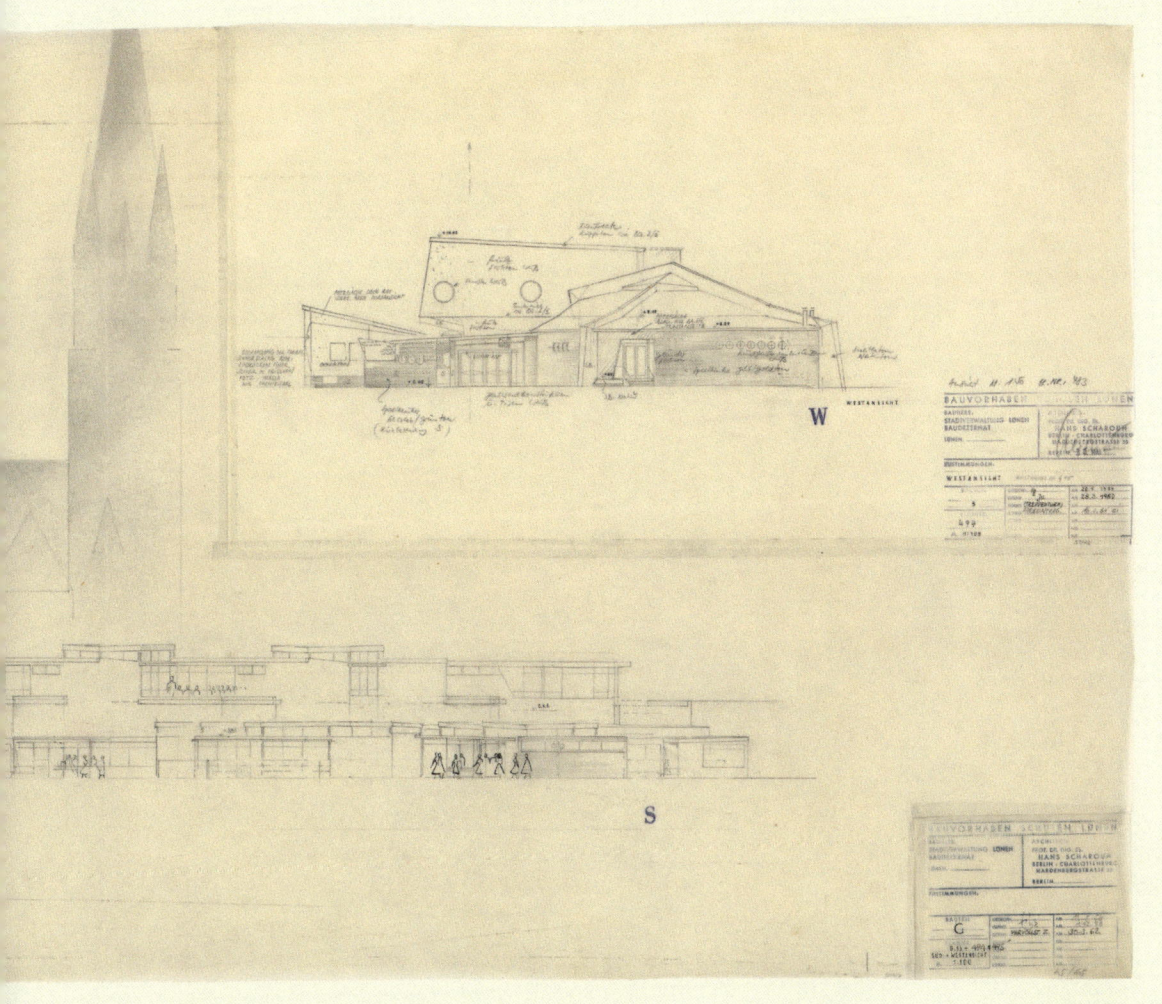

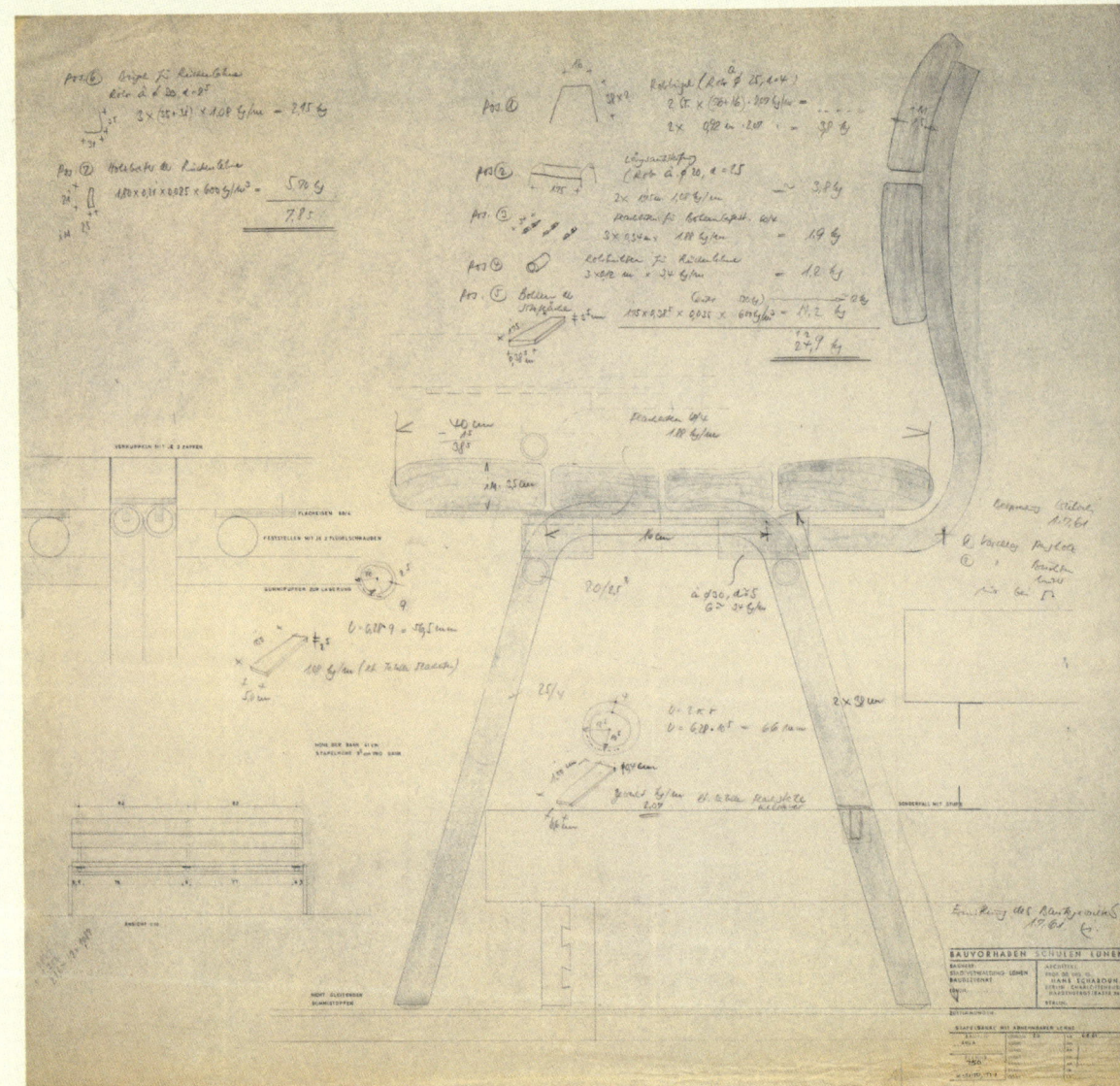

And I think we manage homework much better here, because you can do much more homework in the classroom than you can do in an online class.

> This is completely true because if we're at school and I don't understand an exercise and I don't want to ask the teacher, I can ask my friend and most of the time he explains it way better. And then, after that, I understand it, but in homeschooling there wasn't my friend next to me to explain it to me.

We're learning Spanish from the 11th grade, and we started the 11th grade in homeschooling. And that was very, very hard because we had to talk to each other to learn better Spanish. To learn how to pronounce it better. And, for example, we would talk to our partner in the first five or ten minutes of the lesson and present them something or introduce ourselves, like "My name is..." etc. In online classes it was so hard.

Assembly and Protest:
Parliament and Street

The assumption that adolescence is autonomy without representation is evidently in crisis. Teenagers no longer wait until they can vote to make their voices heard, and secondary education is the place and the moment to assemble, to protest, to occupy, to self-manage. The positioning of bodies in the assembly hall still organises the political spectrum, but new modes of organisation and politicisation are migrating to the classroom, and some are learned there. How are the classrooms occupied, and how do learning spaces change the forms of protesting and assembling? And how does the street become a parliament between the classrooms?

Inner City Arts

Michael Maltzan Architecture, Los Angeles (California), United States, 2008, area: 4,000 m²

How does this building bring together "other classrooms"?

Unlike the other schools selected for this exhibition, Inner City Arts is a centre where teenagers from many state schools go after school. Located in Skid Row, in Downtown Los Angeles, it is a kind of oasis in the socially unbalanced urban context where it is situated. The school is subdivided into several smaller buildings arranged along the adjacent streets, protecting an open-air interior space shaded by palm trees. Being somewhat "secured, but not isolated" from the street, it becomes a place of gathering for students, but also for classes from elsewhere.

What distinguishes this "classroom" from a conventional learning space?

Inner City Arts is more than a school devoted to artistic education: above all, it is a place that seeks to use artistic practices to foster personal development. In order to transgress long-established learning practices, both students and teachers from other schools come here to find new ways to study and learn, allowing them to integrate the visual and performing arts into their school day.

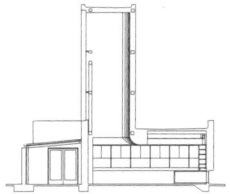

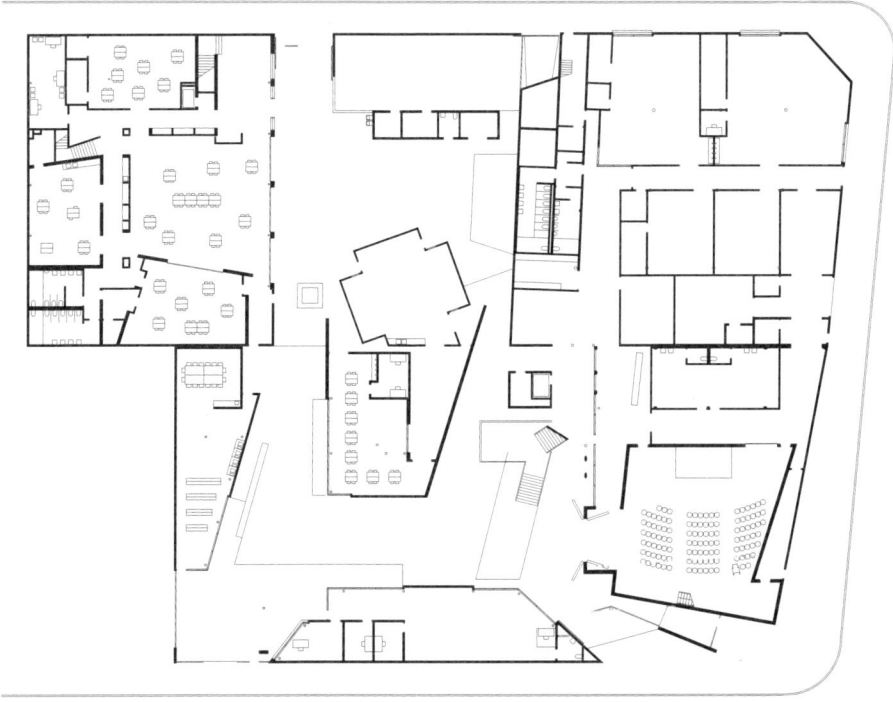

Luís de Freitas Branco High School

Célia Gomes + Machado Costa Arquitectos, Paço de Arcos, Portugal, 2016, area: 17,000 m²

What body politics are deployed in the gathering spaces of the school?

There are more or less formal episodes, which are staged to a greater or lesser degree: there might be a conference or a presentation (the staircase is used as seating for the public, while the mezzanine serves as a balcony), or a graduation ceremony. Sometimes, the space is simply filled with a discussion or a debate about the school itself. There is also a visual reminder of the 1974 Carnation Revolution — a drawing of a red carnation hangs from the top-floor railing, its colour further intensified by the red ceiling — and a staircase where the public gathers to celebrate important events.

What distinguishes this "classroom" from a conventional learning space?

The atrium is simultaneously a square, a spectacular staircase, an audience, a stage and an esplanade, hence its potential to become an assembly space, a place of gathering. Indeed, in the daily life of the school there are so many encounters that can be witnessed: the constant presence of people (those seeking orientation, those coming and going, those staying where they are, those observing); informal encounters (even though there are different routes for teachers, students and staff, everything is done to ensure that they are constantly in contact); or more formal ones (an appointment at the administration office, a request for information at the reception desk, a group of students entering the staff room without knocking, for the good reason that this room does not actually have a door).

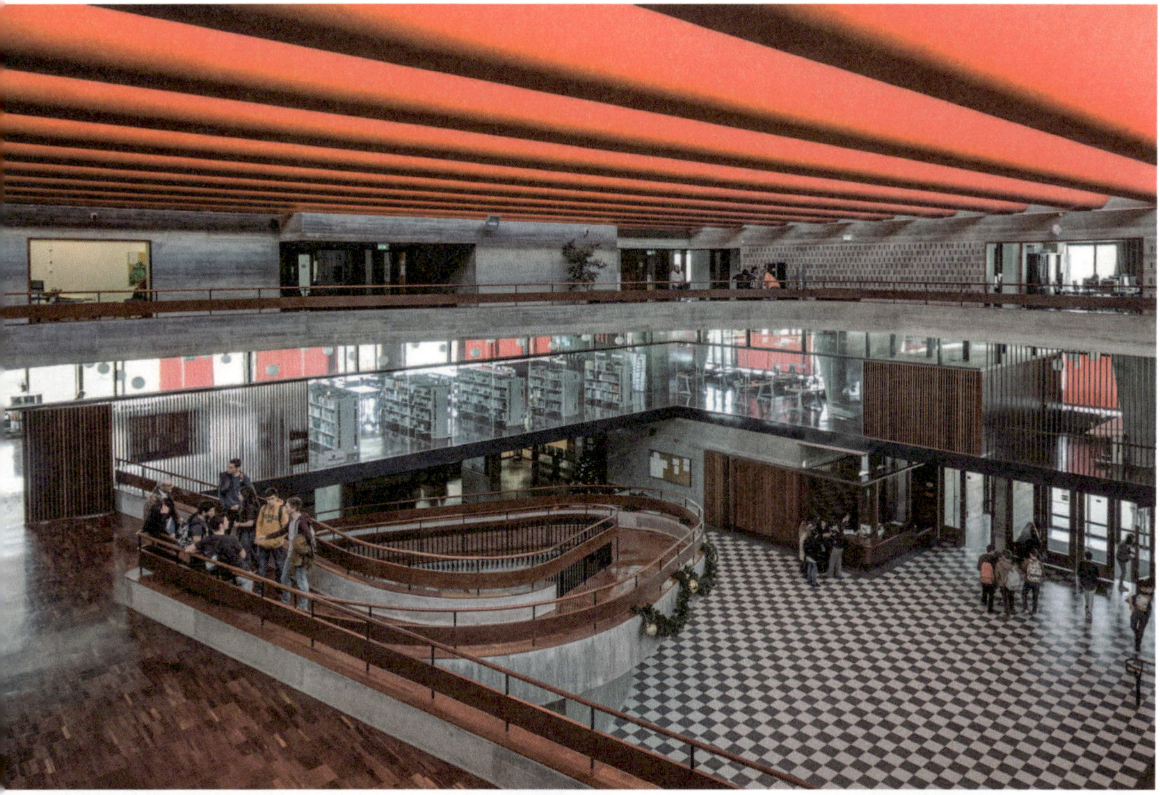

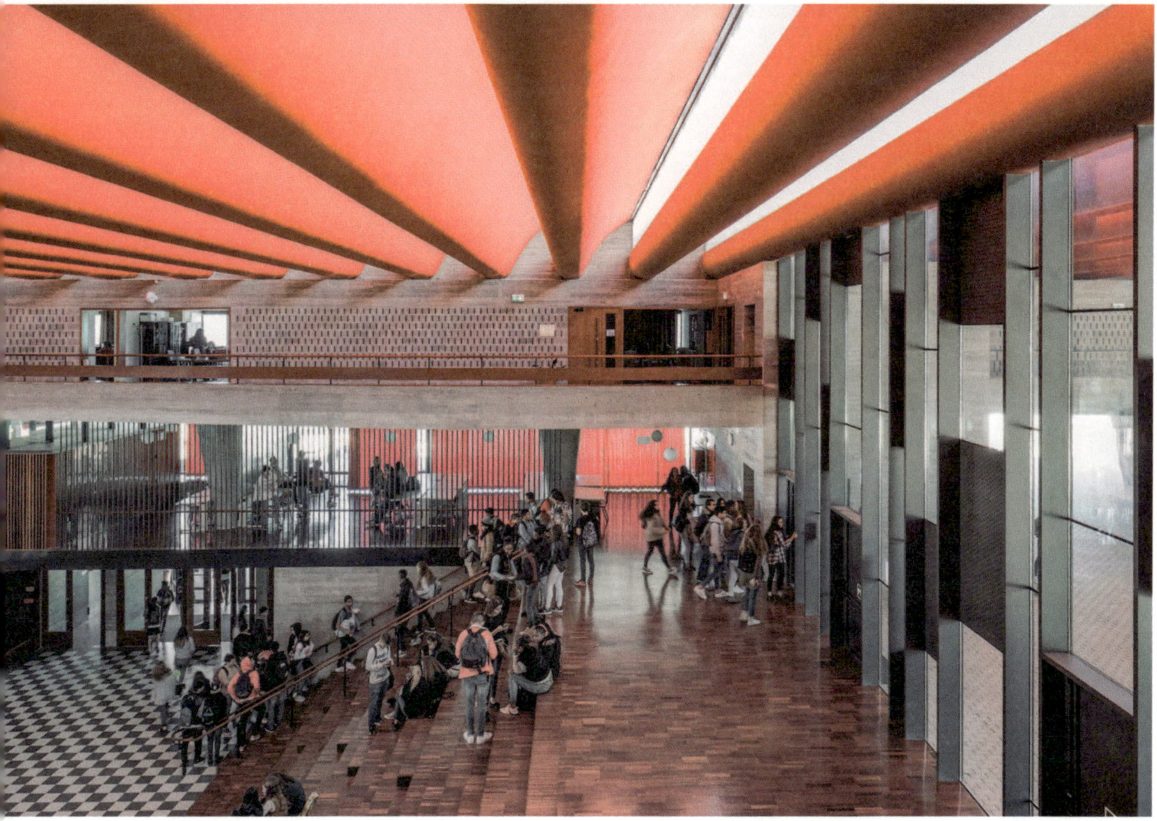

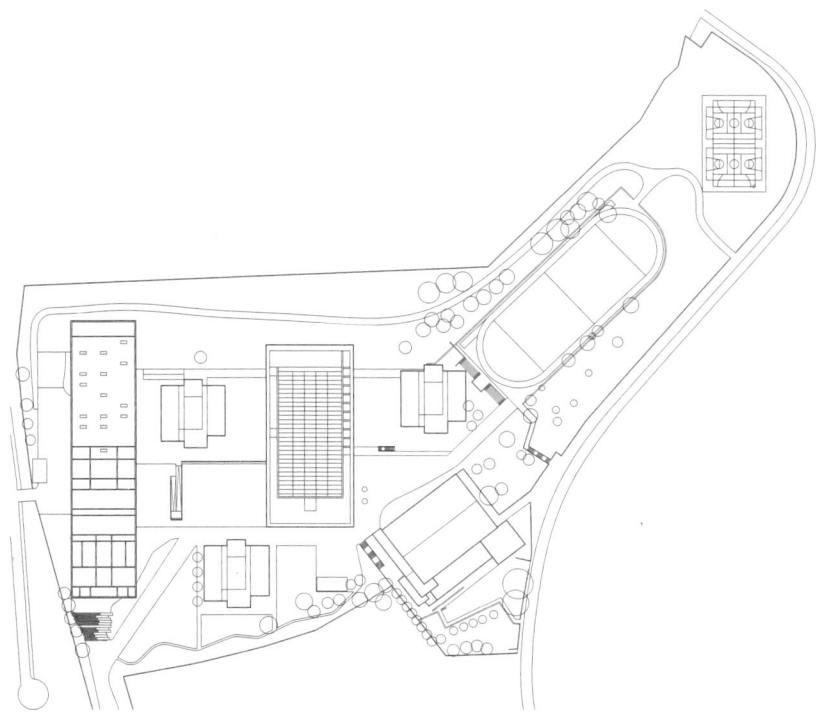

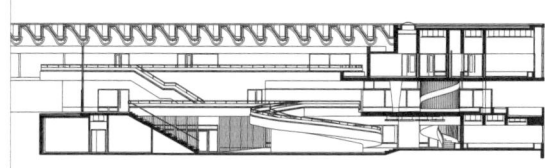

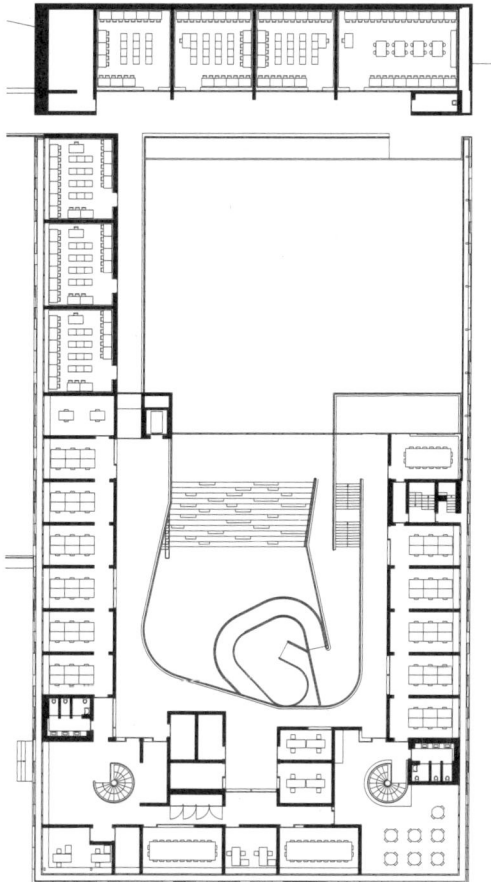

e can, for instance, snack in this room, because it's good. There are
bles, benches, so we can all have a snack here together. Even if
eryone just brings their own food, we have this meeting point.

Transgression

We are normal teenagers like everyone else, we just learn music.

is environment is very welcoming. Many of us have been here since
e were little girls, and that also makes it much more memorable for
. We have lots of
emories from here
d from this environ-
ent; we have a place
re where everybody
ts together. We may
have many differ-
ces, and we each
ve our own pecu-
rities, but we all get
gether and we're all
the same place, and
at makes us all have
mething in common,
d I think that's very good.

Art education can sometimes constitute a counter-field to conventional
teaching. The spaces it occupies — like workshops, amphitheatres or
music rooms — can become islands of freedom and expression in these
ecosystems, and even spaces of transgression and civic disobedience.
This is the case of the Calouste Gulbenkian Conservatory in Aveiro,
Portugal. It was built in the 1960s, based on Maria Noémia Coutinho's
thesis and elaborated under the supervision of architect Carlos
Loureiro. As one of the areas that evaded strict governmental control,
this was an island of freedom built around disciplinary plurality and a
large room with a central fireplace.

There's the bar over there, where we can go for
a snack. We snack there, but we don't have
lunch.

The choir classes stopped because we couldn't all sing by video call, but the teacher would schedule a class once in a
while, just to talk, and he would say: "Study this, this and this piece". But we ended up doing something interesting: each
one sang, then sent in the audio. They put all the audios together and made a video with the theatre, and it was funny...
but we didn't have choir classes. We had musical training too, but it was harder because we also sang in musical training,
and because it was by call it turned out to be difficult, and the instruments and the sound weren't so clear either. With
my instrument, I went to class, the teacher told me to study certain pieces, and during the week I would send him an
audio of the pieces. Then, in the next class, we talked about things to improve. But it was much harder.

There's the orchestra, for instance, where people play instruments. I
play, for example, the bevel flute, and the bevel flute isn't included in an
orchestra. Then we have the ensemble class, and we have IP (which
means Instrumental Practice) where we play other instruments, so we
can have that experience. It's more difficult for some.

e recording system that was being talked about, in my instrument **129**
ss: I always used those recordings. If, for some reason, I couldn't go
class, or the teacher couldn't be present, the teacher always asked
to send a recording to make up for lost time, so at least that part
n't change at all. I got used to that.

Yes, there are also several students who are friends, and, for example, at secondary school, if they didn't follow music, they would end up making a band together, four or five people, and they would play somewhere in Aveiro.

Conservatório de Música Calouste Gulbenkian
Maria Noémia Coutinho, José Carlos Loureiro, Luís Pádua Ramos
Aveiro, Portugal, 1966–71

José Carlos Loureiro was commissioned to design the Calouste Gulbenkian Conservatory in Aveiro, and the project had two main aims: firstly, to decentralise artistic education, and secondly, to make the arts converge by bringing together dance, music and the visual and performing arts within a single secondary school. The commission transgressed the centralism of the specialised educational offer, which was concentrated in Lisbon, and it broke down the walls between the different artistic disciplines. Maria Noémia Coutinho seized the opportunity as the subject for her CODA (Competition to Obtain the Diploma of Architect) in 1966. The numerous forms of play illustrated by Bruegel in his painting *Children's Games* inspired the organisation of the school.

The more public area connects the entrance space with the auditorium, the library and the large multi-purpose hall for ballet, chamber music or exhibitions. The more private area, arranged around the cloister, includes a canteen and rooms for music, painting, sculpture and dance, as well as a common room with a suspended fireplace that was only lit on Saint Martin's Day. The considered robustness of the materials (concrete, painted plaster, wood and bricks) has averted the need for any major works at the school, right up to the present day. It may have lost its kindergarten and moved to an articulated system (whereby conventional education is separated from artistic education, the latter of which takes place in different, specialised schools), yet it still celebrates the marks of time with its worn-down floors and art room tables splattered with paint. It deserves to be listed and to undergo a careful restoration, so that it can keep transgressing both its and our limits.

I think we make a better connection because there are also classes where there's just us and the teacher. In school, there's the whole class and the teacher, so the teacher doesn't focus on one student, they focus on the class. Whereas here, our teacher focuses on us.

I think that the difference between a normal
school and an arts school is that when I come
here, to the conservatory, I dedicate myself
100%: I am myself, I bring my whole world with
me, that's what I mean. Here I am much freer,
and I do the things I like; at the normal school
I'm more reserved.

For example, we learn other instruments. Here in the conservatory, we have one instrument, and
we don't have the opportunity to play two instruments. But then we have classmates who do
play other instruments, and they teach us some things about their instrument, so we can learn a
little bit.

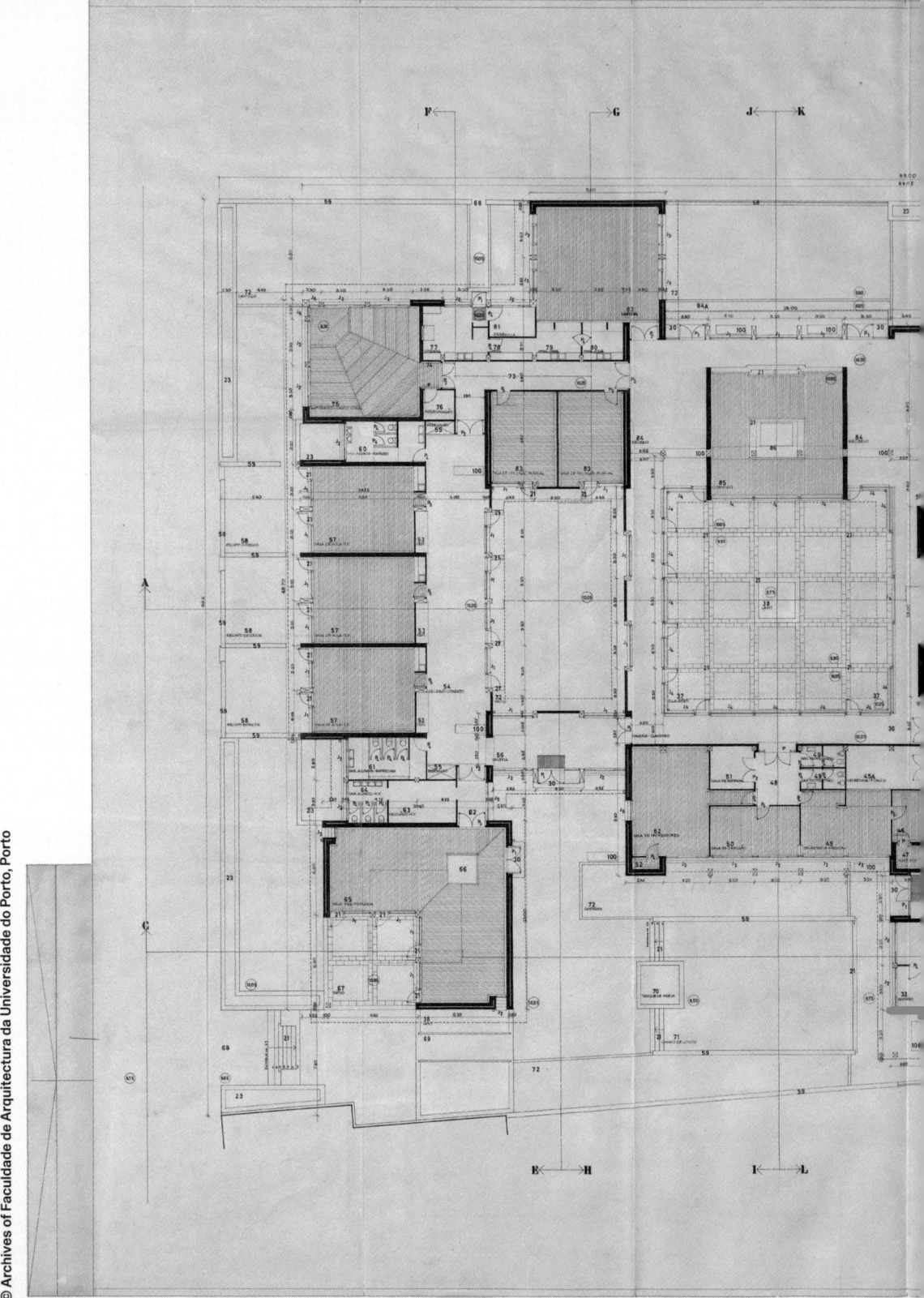

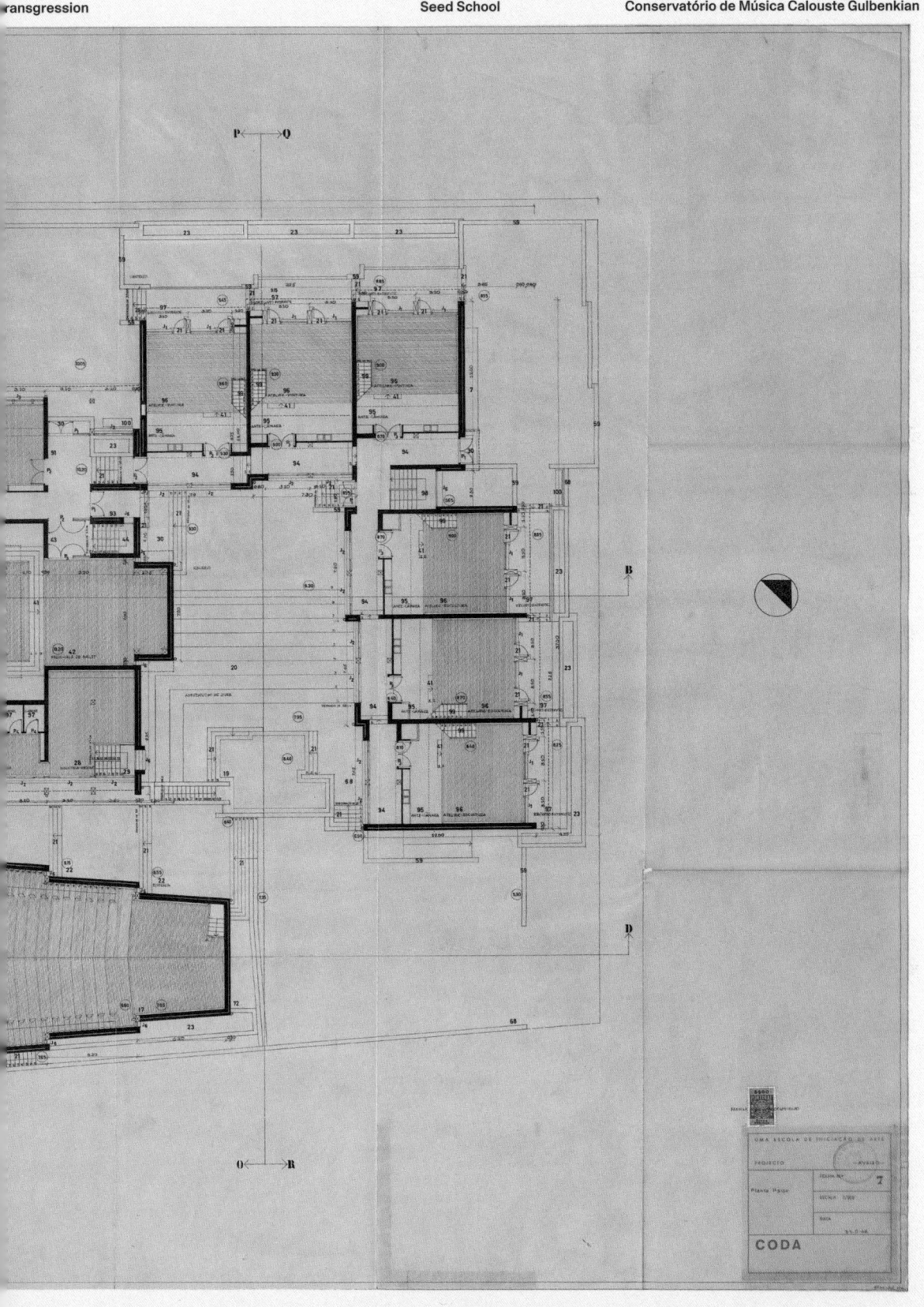

CODA

We had the choice, we were the ones who decided to come here […], while in a normal school it's compulsory […].
But we wanted to come here because we wanted to explore the music part, or the part of the arts, and now there's even
dance […], but the fact that we can choose to come here and choose the subjects, as well as the instruments that we
have here, the ones that we want, is so important. Meanwhile, at school, what we want is already defined.

136

We don't even have the option. We don't need to bring anything special because coming here is
the special thing.

UMA ESCOLA DE INICIAÇÃO DE ARTE
PROJECTO
—AVEIRO—
Corte C-D
FOLHA Nº
14
ESCALA 1/100
DATA
CODA

5$00
PORTUGAL
UMA ESCOLA DE INICIAÇÃO DE ARTE
PROJECTO
—AVEIRO—
Corte O-P
FOLHA Nº
18
ESCALA 1/100
DATA
31-5-66
CODA

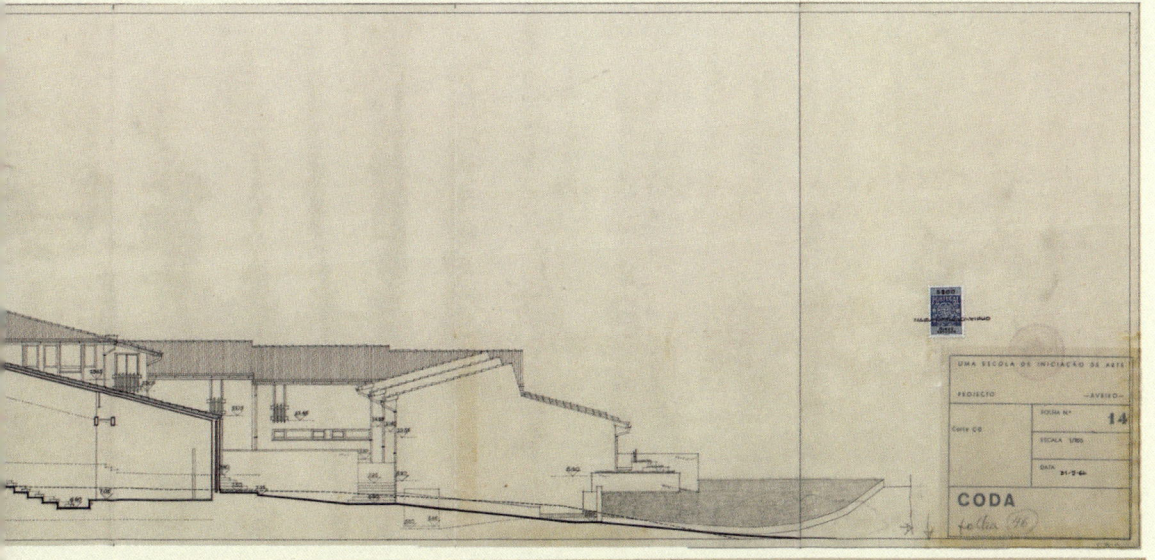

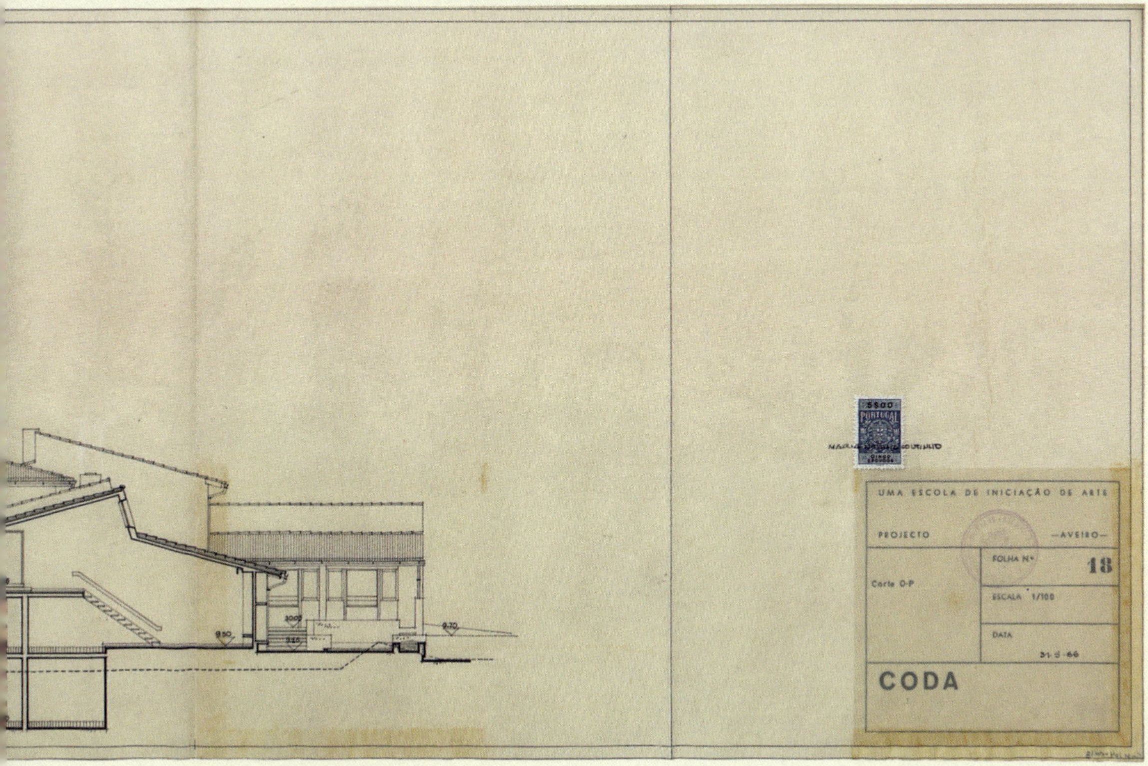

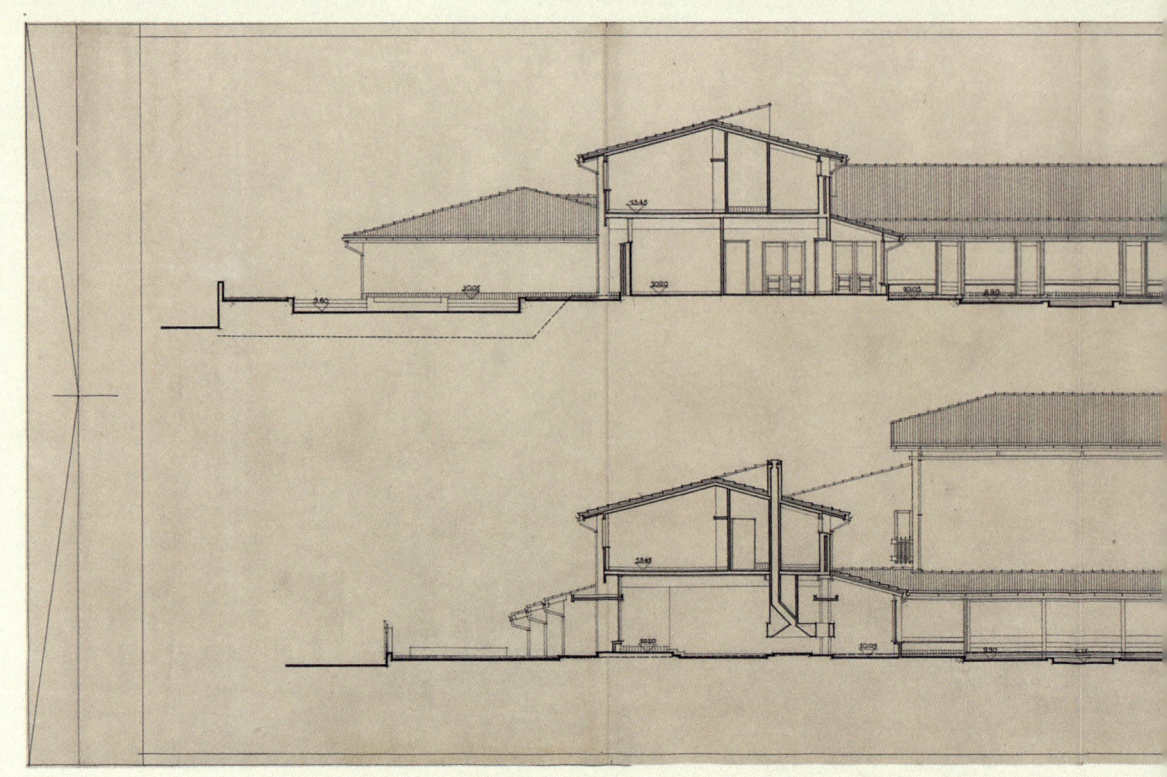

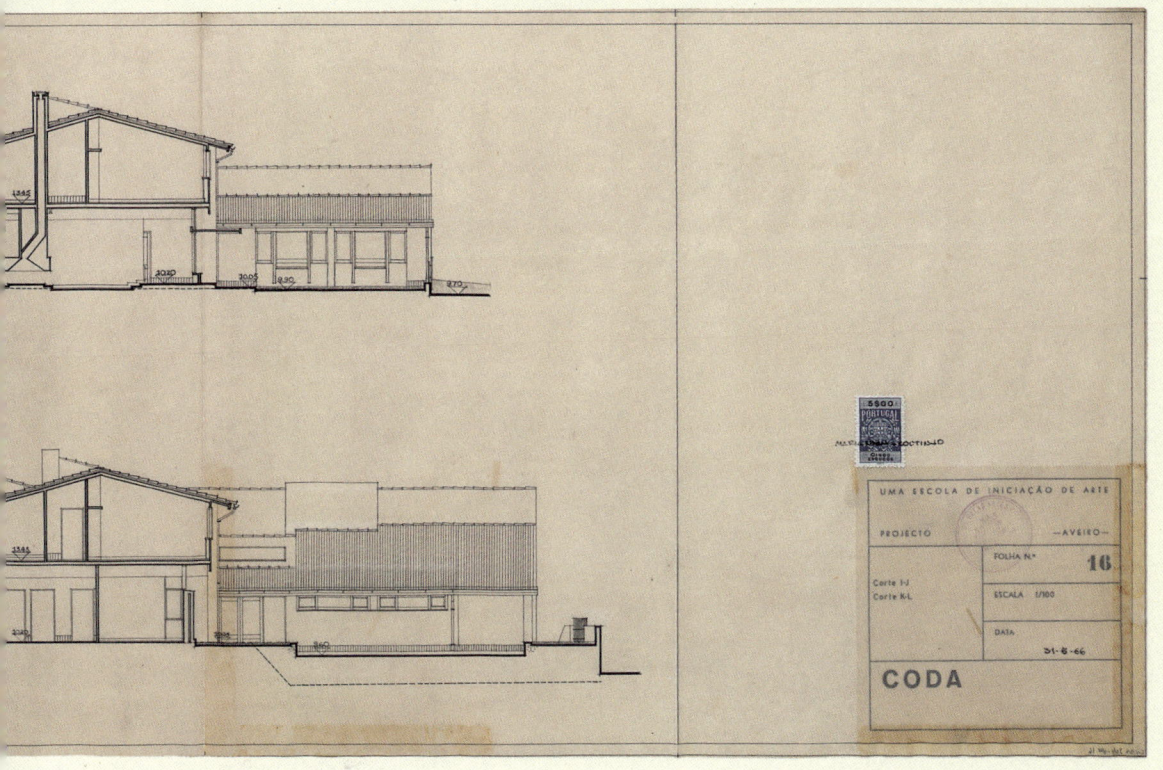

think school prepares us for work: it gives us the skills and also the
mulus. Group tasks stimulate us to work with others, to work in
ams, and to prepare us for the real world, but maybe there are more
eas that include other skills that we don't learn so much at school.

        I think that this is where the connection with
the teacher (that we were talking about before)
is important. The way teaching is carried out
does prepare us [...], because they end up
sharing with us what they've been through,
and it's very important that we hear other
people's experiences to be able to make our
own decisions, to see how other people's pasts
can influence our future.

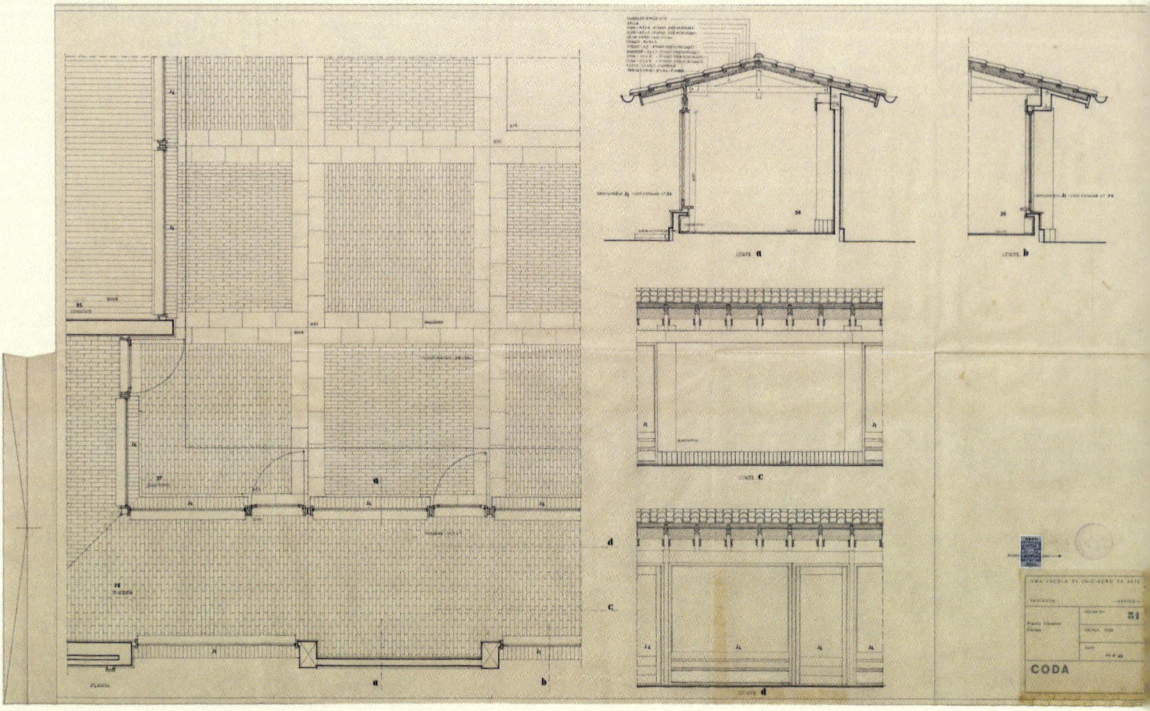

In school, the practical side is also lacking. For instance, I have a cousin in France who did an internship, and that internship gave her an idea of the career she might want to follow, it's experience. Here, in music, that doesn't happen: we get the opportunity to go and play somewhere, to talk to our teacher, to live that experience, but their area is music, so if you don't want to pursue music, you don't really know what to do.

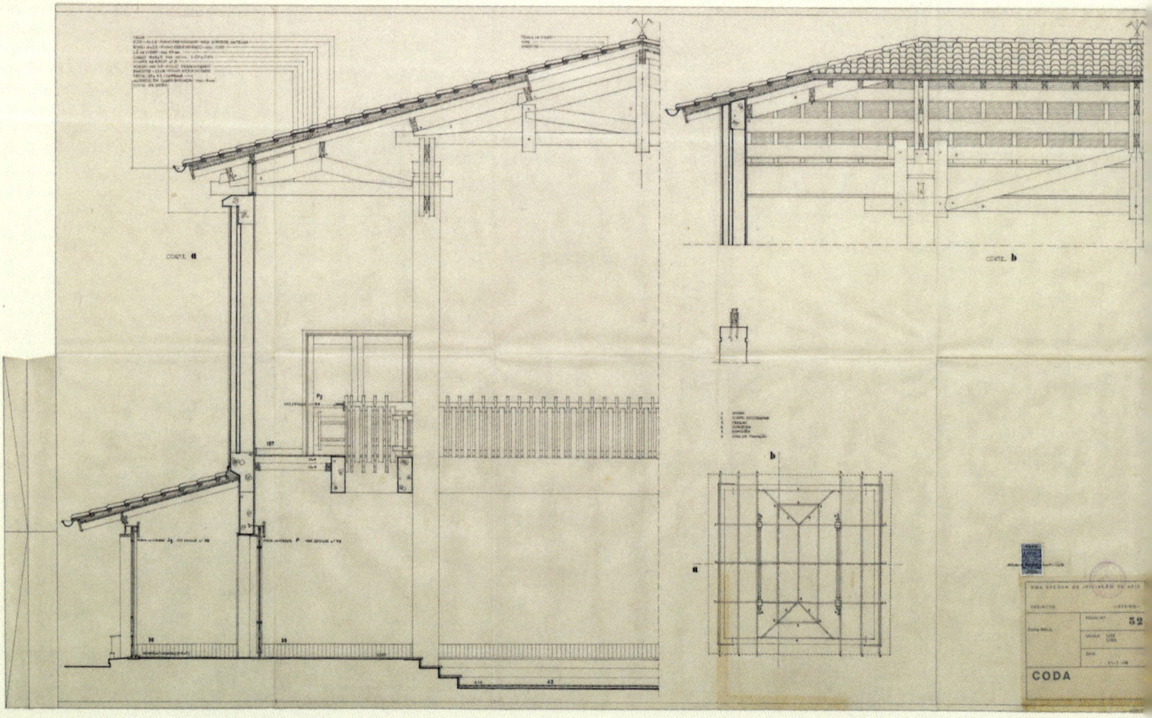

Transgressing Limits and Norms: Atelier and Concert Hall

Transgressing—that is, constantly questioning and challenging the status quo, and the limits and norms it imposes—is the only way for the classroom to become a space where freedom can be enacted. But evading such limits and normativity requires intense self-reflection about how to remap the fluid, dematerialised borders of the classroom, or how to handle the blurring of the limits between disciplines.

Rodrigues de Freitas High School

Manuel Fernandes de Sá, Porto, Portugal, 2007–08, area: 24,000 m²

Can the high school auditorium be considered a classroom?

By a happy coincidence, Manuel Fernandes de Sá, who renovated and designed the extension of this historic school, is also very much involved in the urban planning of Porto. The city's music conservatory, located on the street perpendicular to the high school, holds public concerts in its auditorium. It also has a shop and several rooms that can be transformed into a jazz club. Thinking of art education itself as a form of transgression, and facing the other (i.e. the public), are fundamental parts of the educational process.

What distinguishes this "classroom" from a conventional learning space?

To say that an auditorium can also be a classroom is to question and rethink both typologies. The architectural solution here is rather discreet: the stage is not raised, and is larger than the part set aside for the public. In this arrangement, the stage is the main space and, being a "classroom", it is designed in such a way that the musicians (who are actually students) can listen to each other, even better than the audience.

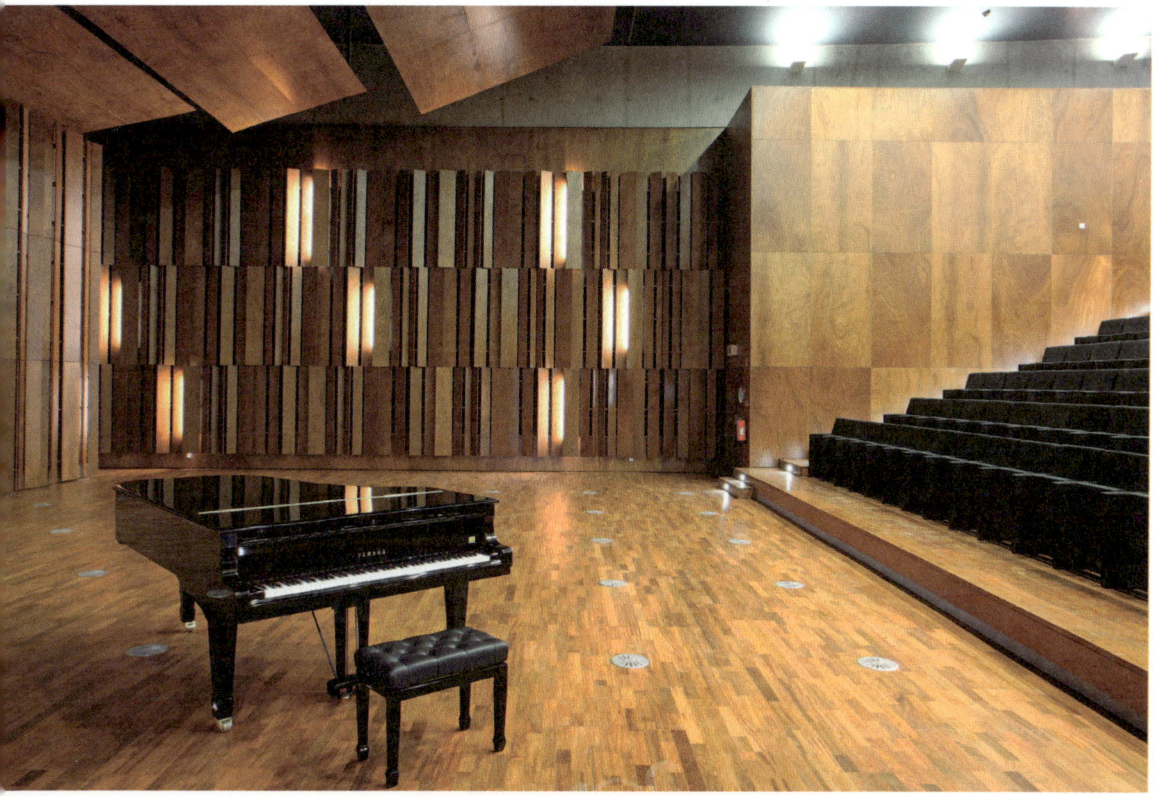

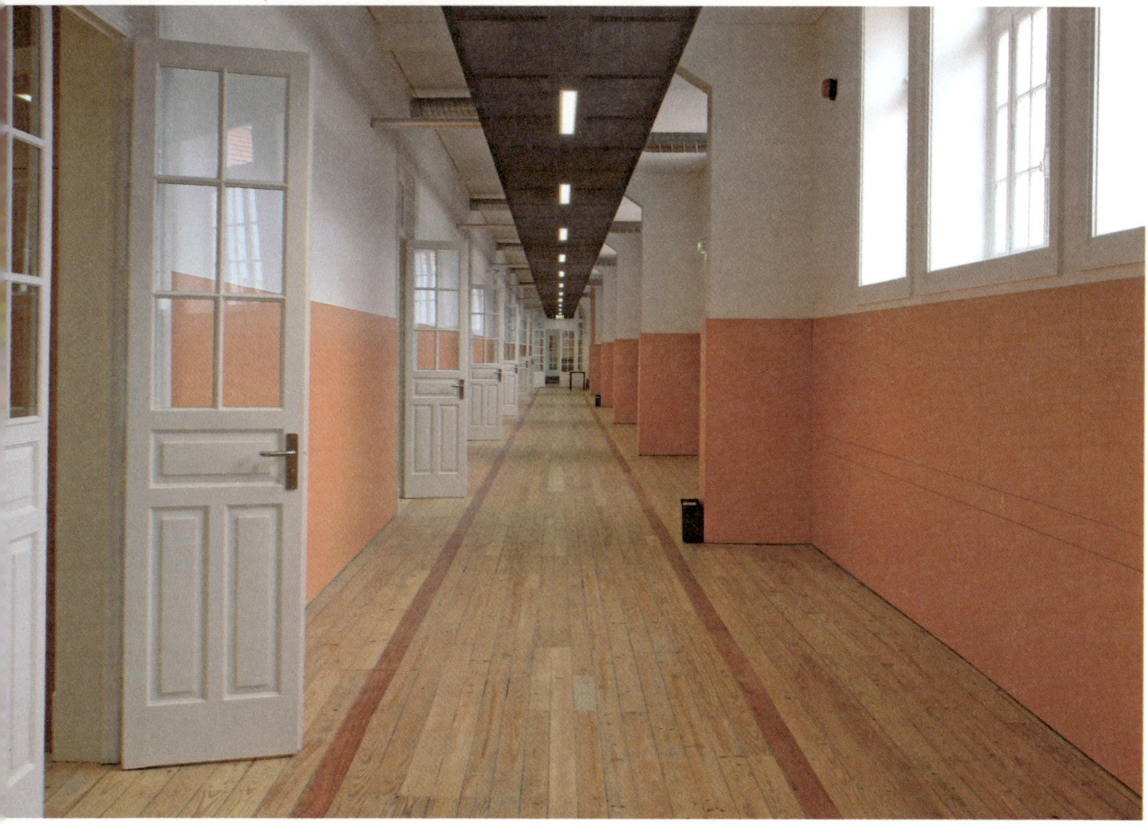

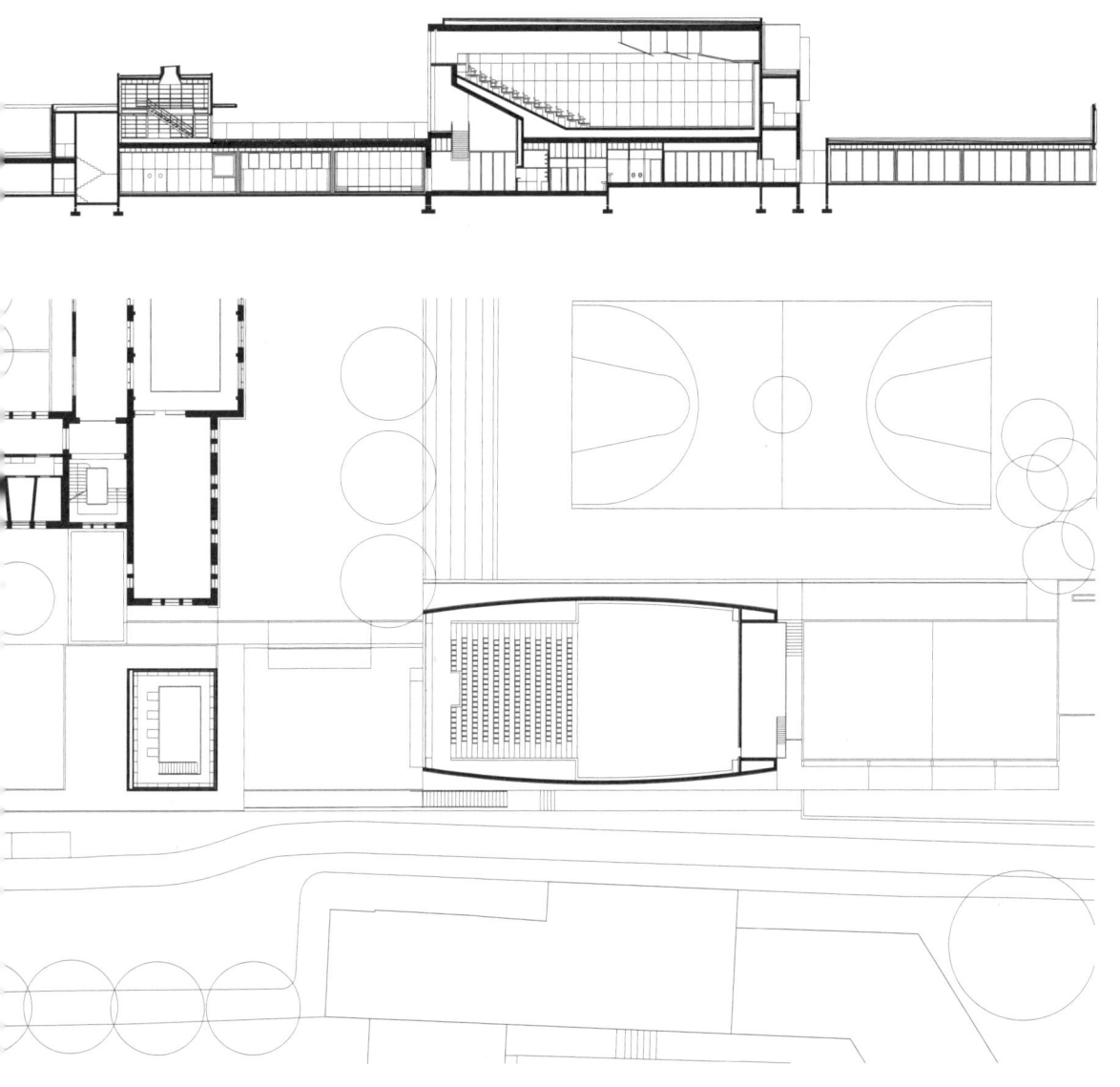

Ørestad High School

3XN architects, Copenhagen, Denmark, 2007–17, area: 12,000 m²

How are new media creating a new type of "classroom"?

Art is a form of transgression that constantly breaks with established habits and practices. Thus, learning an art form is as much about mastering specific skills, instruments and techniques as it is about questioning them, challenging them and inventing new ones. In short, the most difficult task is, as bell hooks put it, "learning to transgress". Students are encouraged to become creators of knowledge rather than passive consumers. New media, being 'new' and largely dematerialised, ensure faster access to places outside the classroom, even away from the school building. In order to anticipate this shift, or at least keep up with it, the architecture has to propose built forms that respond to the constant transformation of informal modes of expression.

What distinguishes this "classroom" from a conventional learning space?

The Ørestad High School has no classrooms, but rather open study environments, where all learning materials are digital. The building is arranged into four open levels, with a large void in the middle, spiral staircases and a sort of covered, vertical communal space. There are no walls, only glass partitions to maintain visual contact at all times. The most radical example of the dematerialisation of the classroom is the existence of a television studio, run entirely by the students, which broadcasts "airborne" parts of the learning experience to the rest of the school community.

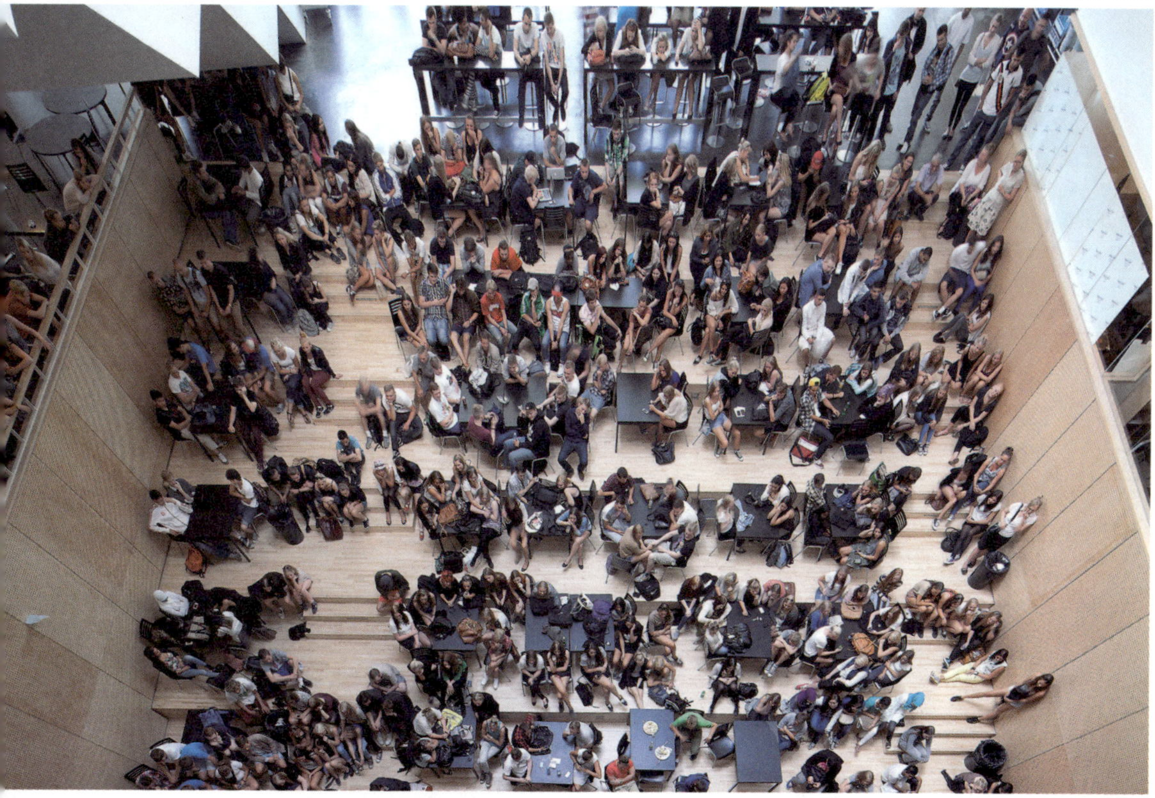

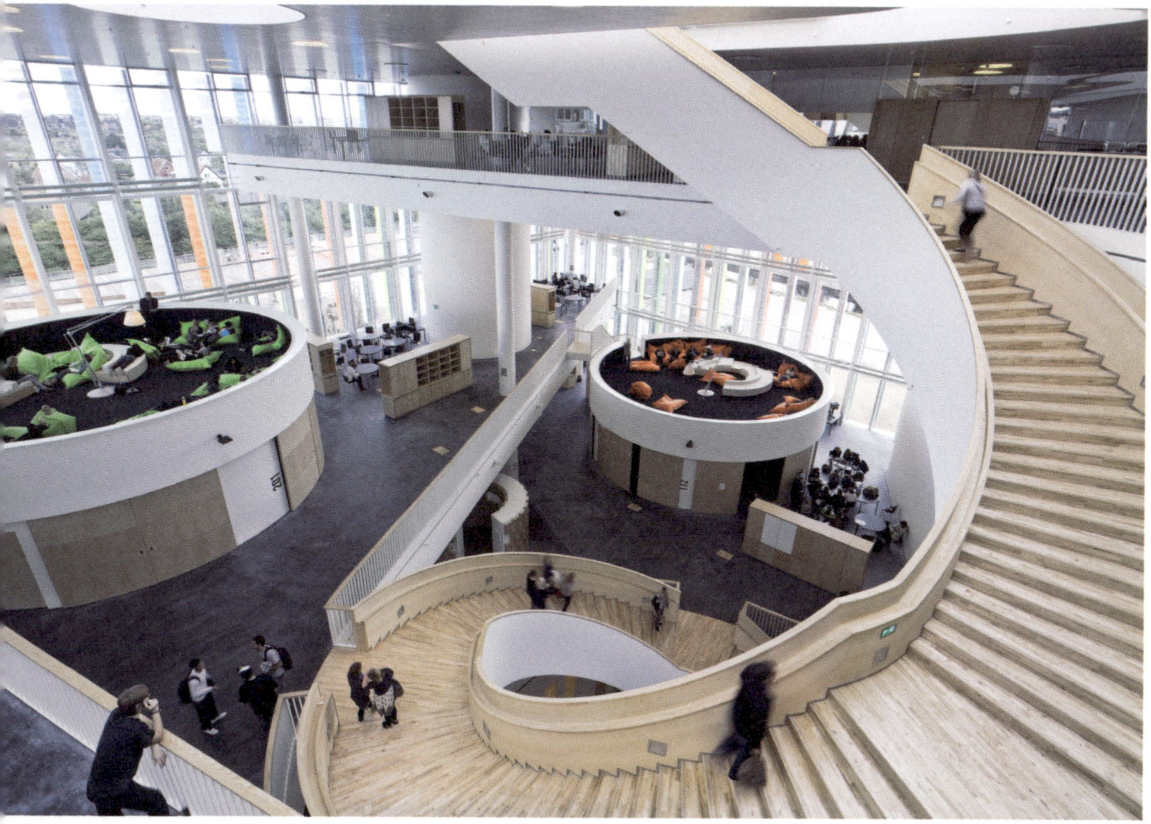

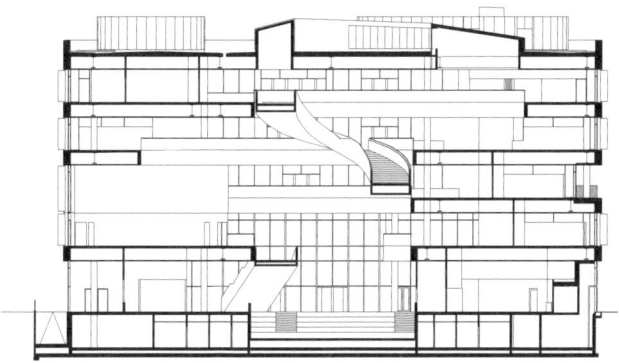

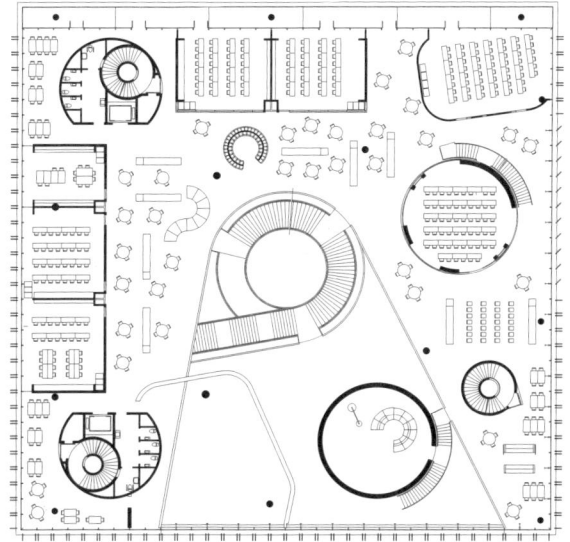

Niekée

LIAG architects and engineers, Roermond, Netherlands, 2007, area: 7,900 m²

What is an "invisible classroom"?

The use of new media allows adults, but also teenagers, to work anywhere. Inside a building, the new classroom can therefore be transformed into a vast open space, with small cocoons where students interact with each other and with the teacher. The school-at-home approach, which became popular during the Covid period, has given many schools a considerable boost in terms of distance learning, based on these media. For Niekée, the idea that "the learning space can be anywhere" has been paramount since the beginning. We changed the concept of the classroom to that of the "zone" or "area", and these different zones are then combined into larger multifunctional spaces. The idea is that children can pick the environment that best suits the given task at hand. As a result, there is a wide variety of spaces, available for learning as an individual, as a group or as a whole class. The spaces can also accommodate even larger groups of students who might come to learn from an inspiring specialist in a particular subject.

What distinguishes this "classroom" from a conventional learning space?

The invisible classroom can be anywhere. It comes down to how the students want to learn, and the kind of group setup they want to work in, depending on the subject being taught. These classrooms are therefore different from the norm because the very notion of the classroom, its conventions and the hierarchical system it implies, are greatly challenged. This school specialises in technology and economics, but the learning takes place in a project-based environment, where students come up with ideas and find creative ways to put them into practice. The subject areas include construction, metalwork, electrical engineering, graphic design, business and sales management.

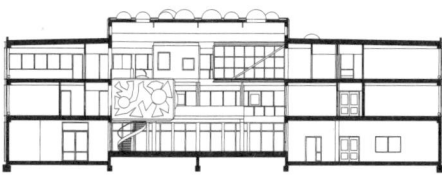

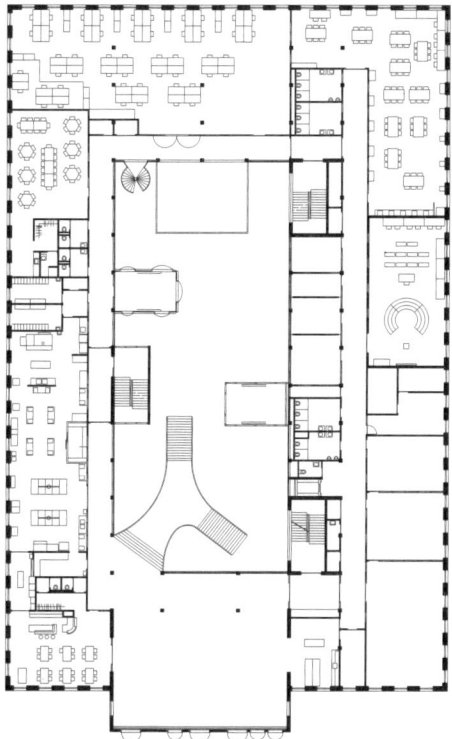

Cheré Botha School

Wolff Architects, Bellville, Cape Town, South Africa, 2017, area: 10,000 m²

How does this school embrace diversity?

It was designed for a community of neurodivergent learners, with the aim of mutually reinforcing the social skills of one part of the group with the cognitive skills of the other. Considering the largely prescriptive nature of public education, programming a truly inclusive "school for all" involves learning how to transgress norms, expectations and stereotypes; the aim is to embrace diversity so that everyone, in a genuinely inclusive way, can discover an experience of freedom in the learning process.

What distinguishes this "classroom" from a conventional learning space?

The main specificity of this building lies more in its shared spaces than in the classrooms themselves. Because of the specific needs of these two groups of students, teaching has to take place in separate classrooms. Nevertheless, they all benefit, both intellectually and in the development of their social skills, from the interactions outside these formal moments of learning. To deal with the local climate, which affects these groups particularly, the corridors (which are natural places for gathering and interacting) had to be protected from the rain and wind. They were therefore designed to be wider than the classrooms on either side, with an A-frame structure to let in plenty of natural light.

Site plan, section and ground floor
Photos: © Dave Southwood

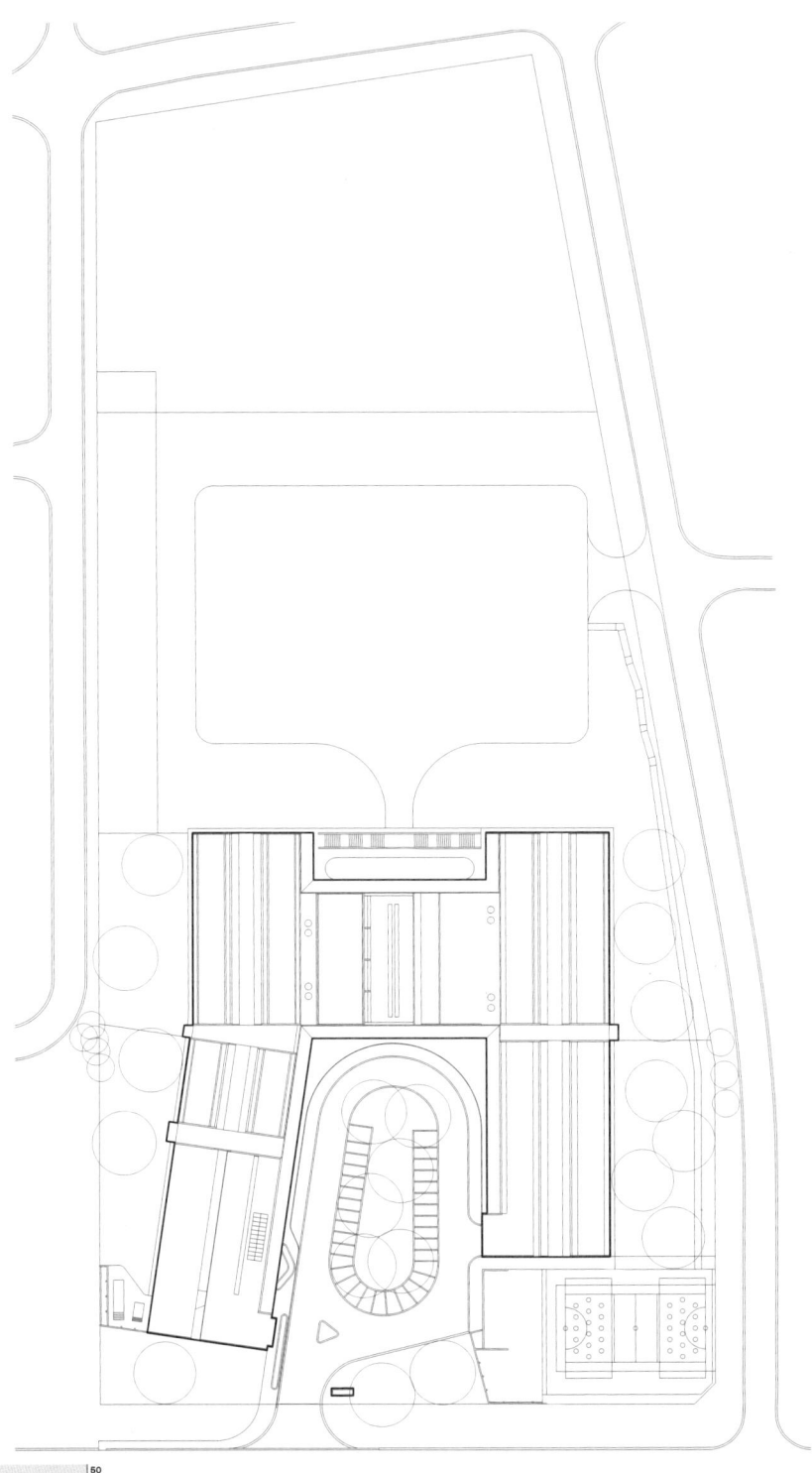

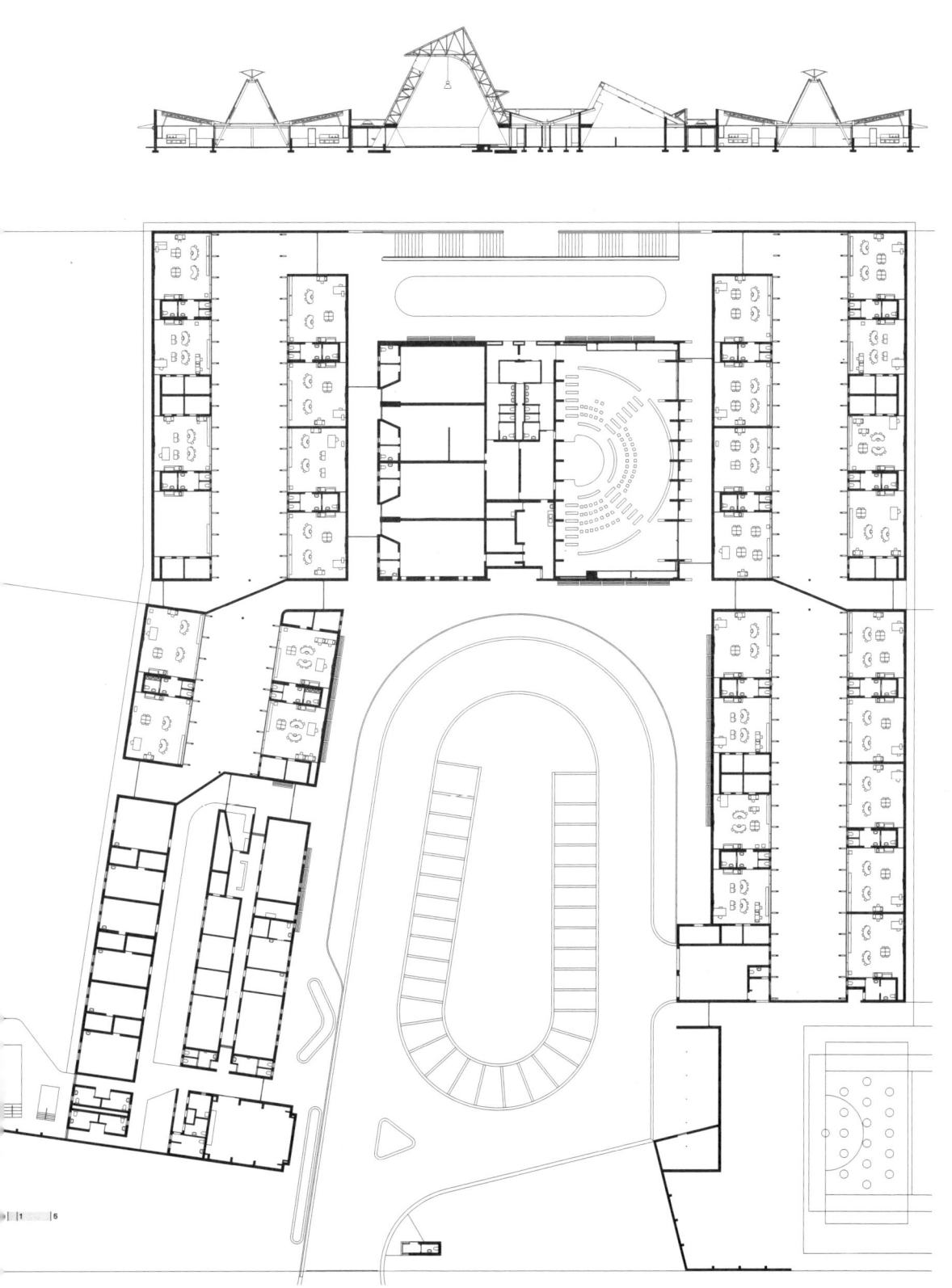

© Luís Leitão

Profession

We hold markets, often a lot of markets, in or outside the school to make it visible. For example, in the courtyard, just outside here, we used to put on small markets. We created products because we could create them in our class. So, we had to have ideas and make them and then sell them. We would invite people from outside the school to come and see what we had made.

**High school—ever divided between the mission of preparing students for higher education, and that of producing workers ready for the labour market—continues its slow mutation. It is trying to keep up with the emergence of a digital economy, while striving, in its modernist attire, to adapt its analogical spaces to these new virtual operations.
The Jean Mermoz vocational high school in Béziers, designed in the 1950s by Pierre Jeanneret, along with Jean Prouvé and Charlotte Perriand, is symptomatic of this evolution. It is a formidable modernist tool, perfectly suited to an industrialised society, and it is now negotiating its passage to the post-industrial digital age.**

have a special room where we can create
projects, so when we have projects, we go
this room. We have all the equipment avail-
le to do whatever we need.

Lycée Professionnel Jean Mermoz
Pierre Jeanneret, Jean Prouvé, Charlotte Perriand
Béziers, France, 1956–59

We also had several internships in different companies.

The need to create a vocational school provided the opportunity to bring together three major names in architectural culture. Pierre Jeanneret conceived the project's functional organisation chart, and later left for Chandigarh. Charlotte Perriand took care of the furniture. Jean Prouvé was tasked with constructing the building, and he tested prefabrication models brought in from the aeronautical industry: aluminium roofs in the shape of aeroplane wings, brise-soleils to shade the façades, and mechanically operated projecting casement windows. The school would adapt to the needs of the labour market of the time by reproducing its different formats (the office, the workshop and the factory), and prefabrication would provide the required flexibility. Standardisation, as might be expected, collided with the material reality of getting things done: a lightweight aluminium structure, for example, was ultimately made from wood.

Contemporary reality has brought with it an unexpected novelty: that is, the digitisation of work, or, in other words, its dematerialisation. From workshops to business schools, learning environments are beginning to be populated by numerical control machines, 3D printers and, everywhere, the Internet, which operates just as much in manufacturing as in promotion or sales. The format for transmitting knowledge, however, is not so different from that of the medieval guilds: knowledge is passed down from masters to apprentices. Here, a mark of this can be seen in the permanence of the person responsible for directing the school, the one who still holds the title of *Proviseur*. This person lives in the central building's rooftop apartment.

 create objects with 3D printers. We also have computers, all kinds ools, laminators too.

This room is called the Fablab. It's available all day long, except in the middle of the afternoon when we have lunch. It's available to everyone, both students and teachers, and everyone can do what they want there, such as flock clothes or aprons. We can create objects there, so it's under demand.

 of this is part of our course. We started with es plans, to familiarise ourselves with the rking world.

© Luís Leitão

To give you an example, it was for the final work of our class. So, we got into groups of two and we had to create a product. There were satin hair scrunchies, aprons, mask bags, so we had a lot of products. And then, to show them to people, we had to go to the main courtyard, right here, so we made little stands with our product posters, and photos with the prices. So, we made a marketplace with the people of the school, both the teachers and the people working here, and we learnt how to sell and market a product.

The school building, as you can see, is inspired by Mondrian, the artist. So, the customers came to see our school, and then we also showed them around if they wanted to, because there are several types of buildings.

ctually, the markets that we held in the school were mostly in the courtyard. This means the ont and back courtyard, at the entrance, and in the multi-purpose room. So, we have several aces to use. We didn't especially do it in classrooms, it was more outside, you know, in the ourtyard, in the entrance. Our markets were at the entrance, so at the car park of the entrance; e good thing was that the customers went directly in front of it, so they could see that there as something going on. It was open to anyone, so those who didn't know about it could see at there was something happening there.

So, there is building D, which is for mechanics, and building C, for boat mechanics. Building D is for carpentry and mechanics, and it also does a little bit of sales, because that's where we have our room for making products.

You can see that it's a plane wing; the school is like that on the B building especially. You can see that all the rooms have different colours for the walls, as it's inspired by Mondrian.

And it's a pleasure because, when we started, we didn't know the school at all, and now we're going to be in our final year and we're the ones showing the school. We know all the places in it, we can talk about it as well, and it's a pleasure too to let other people know about the school.

e have bovine traceability, as marked at the entrance of the canteen, because now it's regu- ed: we know where the products mainly come from. So, we know the origins, not of every- ng, but we know the origins of most of it. We know where the beef comes from, whether from ance or another country, for example. And here we generally try, I think the canteen manager es, to make food of French origin, and sometimes they do organic, vegan menus, or themed enus. For the Erasmus week they had a Spanish menu, that kind of thing. They try to vary pending on the period.

We're the salespeople of tomorrow, so they train us to be operational immediately, but also in ten years' time: we are trained in everything technological, because there will probably be salespeople equipped with a tablet, for example. We will say that we have known the telephone era, the generation before not necessarily, they were one of the first, innovative. So, it's up to us to change our profession.

163

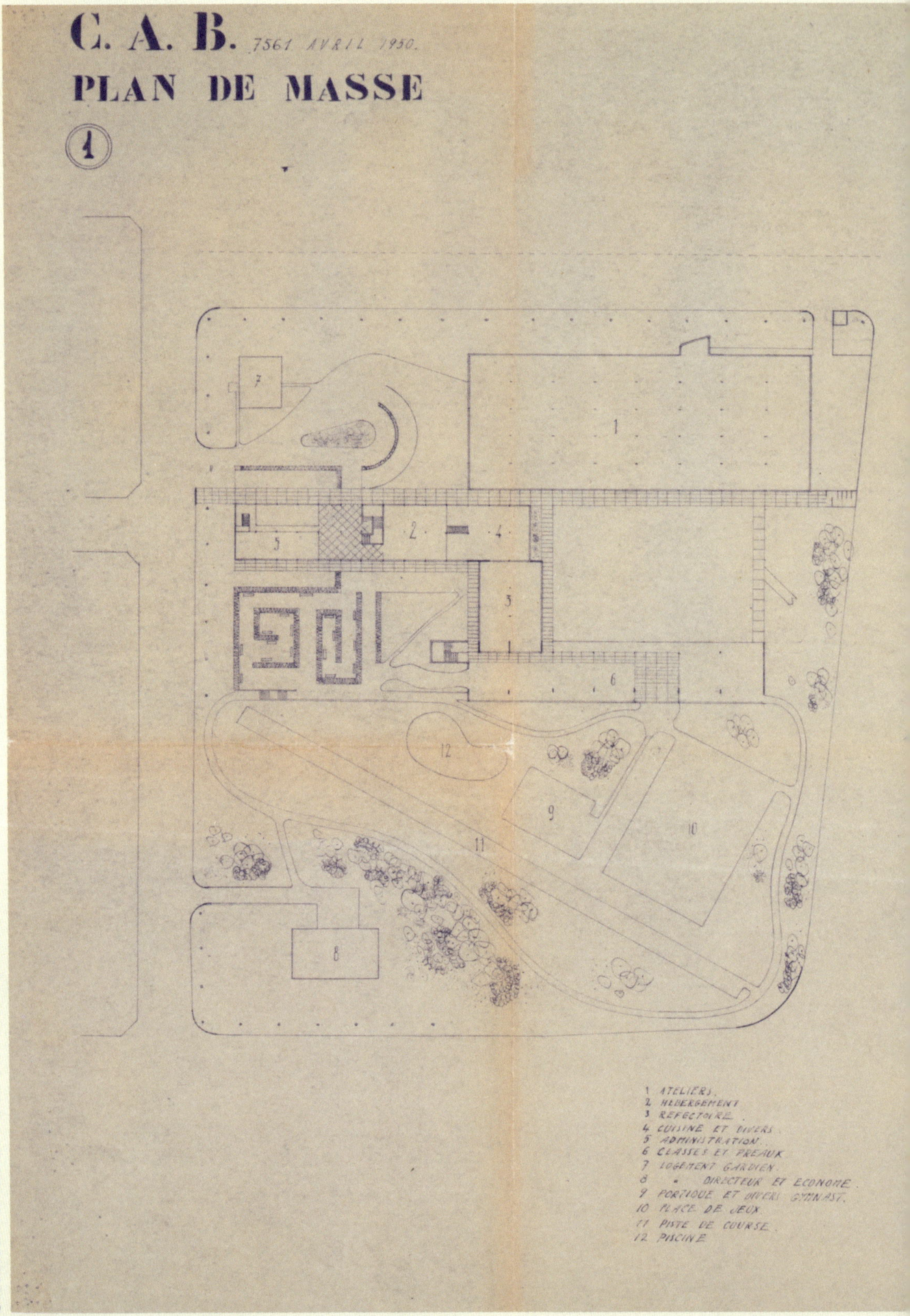

C. A. B. *7561 AVRIL 1950.*
PLAN DE MASSE

1 ATELIERS.
2 HEBERGEMENT
3 REFECTOIRE.
4 CUISINE ET DIVERS.
5 ADMINISTRATION.
6 CLASSES ET PREAUX
7 LOGEMENT GARDIEN
8 " DIRECTEUR ET ECONOME.
9 PORTIQUE ET ABRI GYMNASE.
10 PLACE DE JEUX
11 PISTE DE COURSE.
12 PISCINE

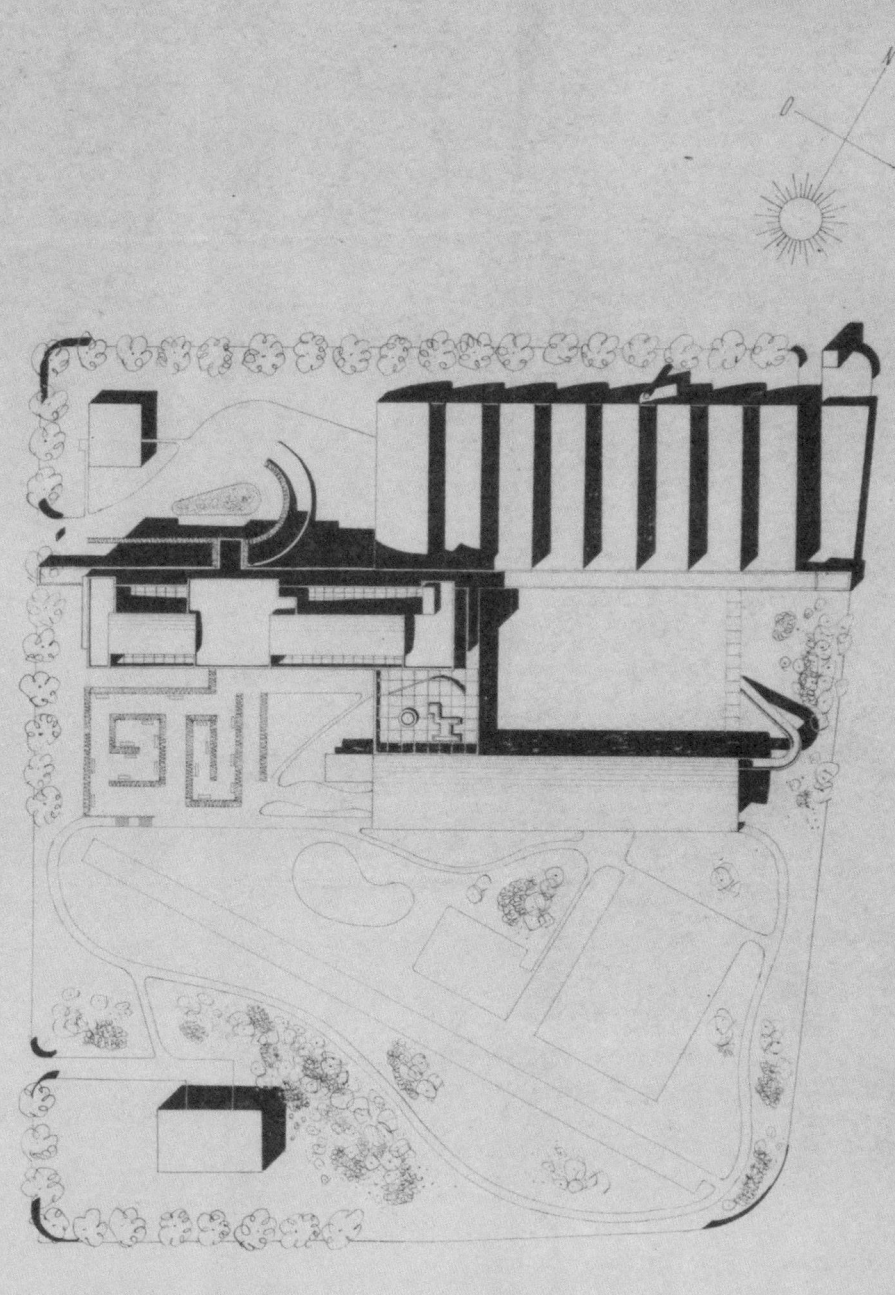

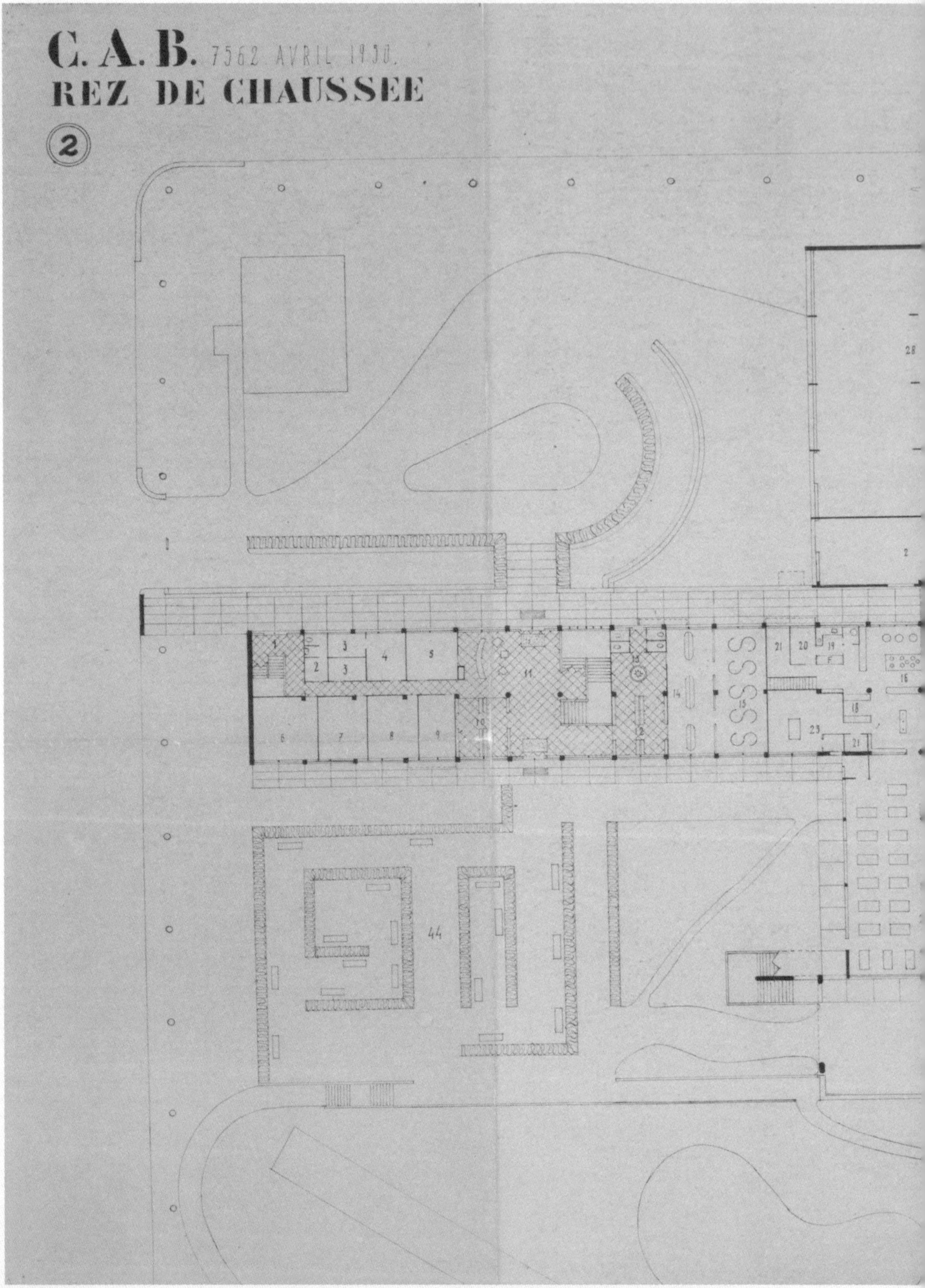
C. A. B. 7562 AVRIL 1950.
REZ DE CHAUSSEE
2
44

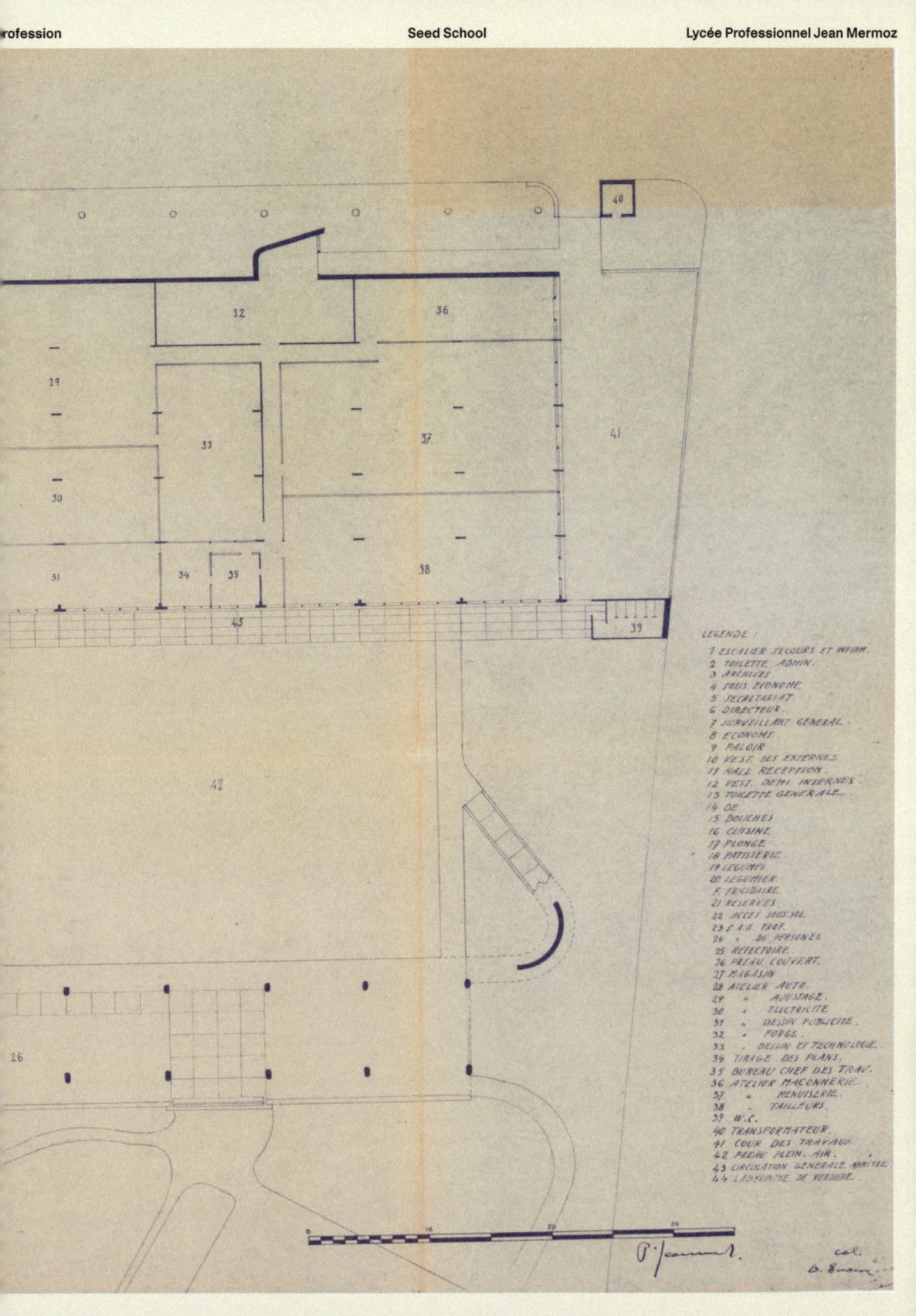

LEGENDE :

1 ESCALIER SECOURS ET INFIRM.
2 TOILETTE. ADMIN.
3 ARCHIVES
4 SOUS ECONOME
5 SECRETARIAT
6 DIRECTEUR
7 SURVEILLANT GENERAL.
8 ECONOME.
9 PALOIR
10 VEST. DES EXTERNES
11 HALL RECEPTION
12 VEST. DEMI INTERNES
13 TOILETTE GENERALE.
14 OIE
15 DOUCHES
16 CUISINE
17 PLONGE.
18 PATISSERIE
19 LEGUMES
20 LEGUMIER.
F FRIGIDAIRE.
21 RESERVES
22 ACCES SOUS SOL
23 F.I.A. PROF.
24 " DU PERSONEL
25 REFECTOIRE.
26 PREAU COUVERT.
27 MAGASIN
28 ATELIER AUTO.
29 " AJUSTAGE.
30 " ELECTRICITE
31 " DESSIN PUBLICITE.
32 " FORGE.
33 " DESSIN ET TECHNOLOGIE.
34 TIRAGE DES PLANS.
35 BUREAU CHEF DES TRAV.
36 ATELIER MACONNERIE.
37 " MENUISERIE.
38 " TAILLEURS.
39 W.C.
40 TRANSFORMATEUR.
41 COUR DES TRAVAUX.
42 PREAU PLEIN. AIR.
43 CIRCULATION GENERALE ABRITEE
44 LABYRINTHE DE VERDURE.

C.A.B.
7565. AVRIL 1950.
5

U D _ O U E S T

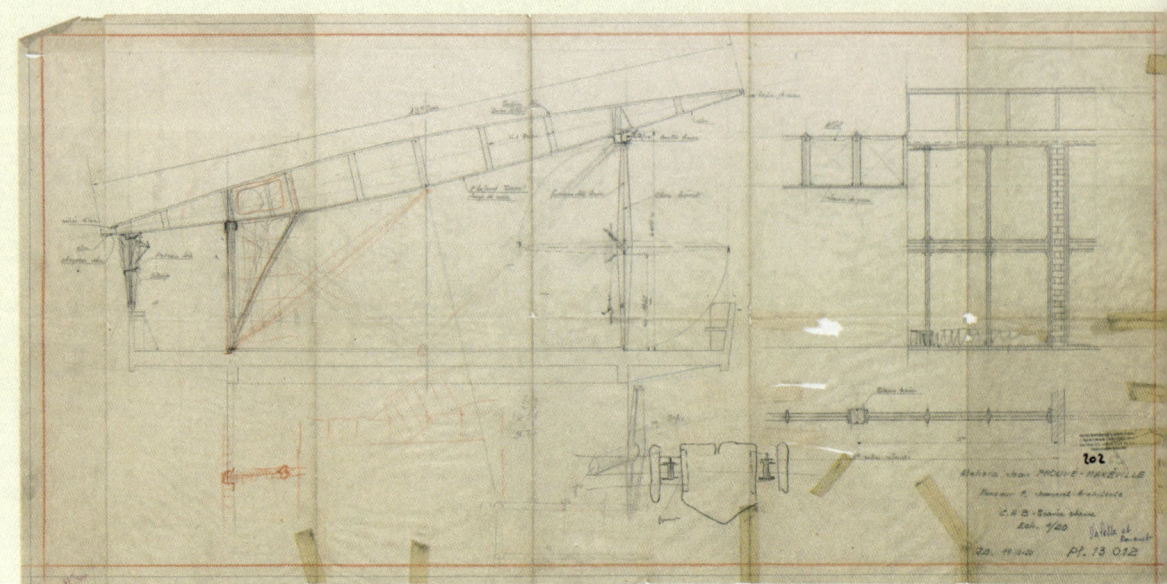

© Archives départementales de Meurthe-et-Moselle, Nancy

We forgot to mention Erasmus, which is a European project. I took the English-Euro option, so I can have two extra hours of English a week to improve my English language skills. So, we have the English-Euro, which allows me to go on trips with Erasmus, three weeks in one of the partner countries, and it is renewed every two years. And then next year they're opening the Spanish-Euro section, so two more hours of Spanish, I suppose. As with English, we'll acquire additional knowledge, and that will be marked on the baccalaureate that we're going to get. The Euro part will feature on the diploma.

We work together a lot. The teachers in the professional environment are much more present: they try to take us as far as possible, and we, as classmates, often work as a team, so we work hard for the markets, for all the projects we have done. We all work together, and this trains us for our future jobs.

The games we played earlier are shared via this software. So, we are trained almost exclusively in digital technology.

Learning to Work:
Office and Workshop

The social role of secondary education is to shape young people into functional adults. On the one hand, secondary education is a portal for higher education, while on the other it fulfils the need (pressingly so) for a well-trained and adaptable workforce, as provided by vocational schools. Paradoxically, work appears to change even faster than education, and here we will inquire into the impact of the close relationship, and often even mimicry, between the classroom and the workshop/office. Is it important, we ask, that the future of work and the future of technical education influence each other? And how is vocational education reorganising the links between work and education?

Dr. Mário Sacramento High School

Inês Lobo Arquitectos, Aveiro, Portugal, 2015, area: 15,662 m²

Is the analogue classroom being updated to accommodate digital work?

Sixty years after the delivery of the original building of this "industrial school" (or technical college), its renovation and extension are an opportunity to rethink the very notion of professional education, both in terms of the nature of the professions it must train in order to meet the needs of today's market, and in the type of professionals it teaches. As a result of changes in the local industrial landscape and greater mobility within the larger territory, this institution — which used to train mainly manual, rather than intellectual workers (i.e. blue collar rather than white collar) — now has to respond to the demands of a larger, more complex and more diversified labour market.

What distinguishes this "classroom" from a conventional learning space?

In terms of the balance between renovation, demolition and expansion, it is clear that the manual skills taught here have remained the same: in relative terms, the workshop space remains broadly the same after the renovation. What changes is the size and, in a way, the functions of the school as a whole; there are new classrooms where additional skills are taught, ranging from foreign languages to computer science to economics. The classroom is thus "expanded" and exists from the constant back-and-forth between the workshop and the more formal classroom.

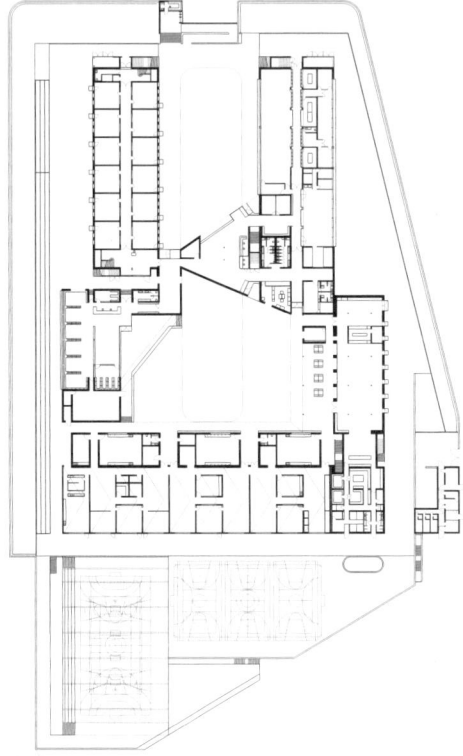

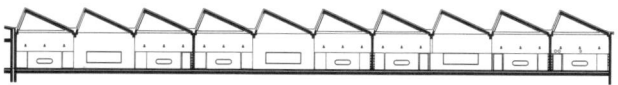

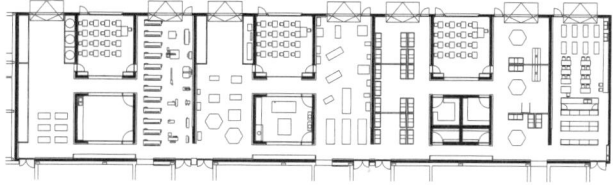

Elishout Kitchen Tower

XDGA – Xaveer De Geyter Architects, Anderlecht, Belgium, 2003–11, area: 3, 300 m²

Can a restaurant be considered a classroom?

As well as learning how to feed others, and how to balance flavours and nutritional contributions, learning to cook also means finding one's place in the sometimes-complex codes and rituals of a communal meal. What's the point of cooking food if no-one eats it? The restaurant is open to the public, and is located on the top floor of a tower stacked with cooking workshops where the students learn and practice. It has a spectacular panorama, and it considers the social act of sharing a meal as the culmination of the whole learning process.

What distinguishes this "classroom" from a conventional learning space?

The name given to the building, Kitchen Tower, is as descriptive as it is intriguing. Like all towers, this one is designed to save floor space, to provide maximum built area with a limited footprint, on an already-dense campus. Like all towers, it is also a landmark, so the campus is visible from the nearby expressway. Each floor is arranged on a square plan, and there is a special kind of teaching laboratory, where the subject taught is the culinary arts. It differs from a traditional classroom, but also from a classic kitchen, because of the multiple cooking and preparation stations: it is a classroom made up of a succession of school kitchens.

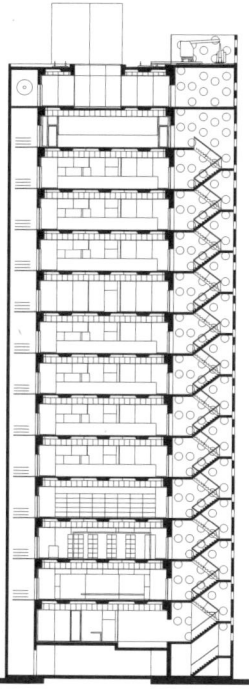

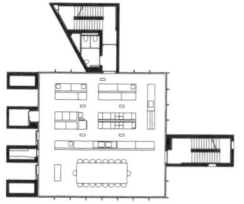

Business Academy Bexley

Foster + Partners, London, United Kingdom, 2003, area: 11,800 m²

Should the classroom simulate the workplace?

For the Bexley Business Academy, Foster + Partners applied the same philosophy as for its office buildings, an approach which pioneered the humanisation of the workplace in the early 1970s. The idea was to design a "business institute" that would engender a sense of institutional pride and community. They sought to challenge the traditional "corridor and classroom" duo by channelling circulation through open balconies and covered atriums, thus creating a more open environment inspired by contemporary workplaces. The classroom design borrows heavily from the design of contemporary workplaces, with rooms that are more open and transparent than traditional teaching spaces, in order to maximise natural light and views. Different types of teaching spaces are thus visually linked throughout the building, producing a general sense of transparency and openness.

What distinguishes this "classroom" from a conventional learning space?

The academy's curriculum places particular emphasis on business, art and technology, driven in part by Bexley's entrepreneurial sponsors. Within the building, these three areas of education correspond to three light-filled interior patios. Three levels of classrooms are arranged around these interior courtyards, resulting in a seamless visual link within each thematic area, which also allows for fluid and natural supervision. On the upper levels, some spaces are open on one side, so that multi-purpose teaching areas with screens can be created within the larger volume. The focal point of the Academy is its large central hall, which is also a flexible teaching area. It overlooks an all-day café, where students can enjoy all their meals, from breakfast to dinner. With close links to the local community, the school's gym (with its climbing wall), café, recording studios and state-of-the-art lecture theatre are all available for hire, or for use outside school hours.

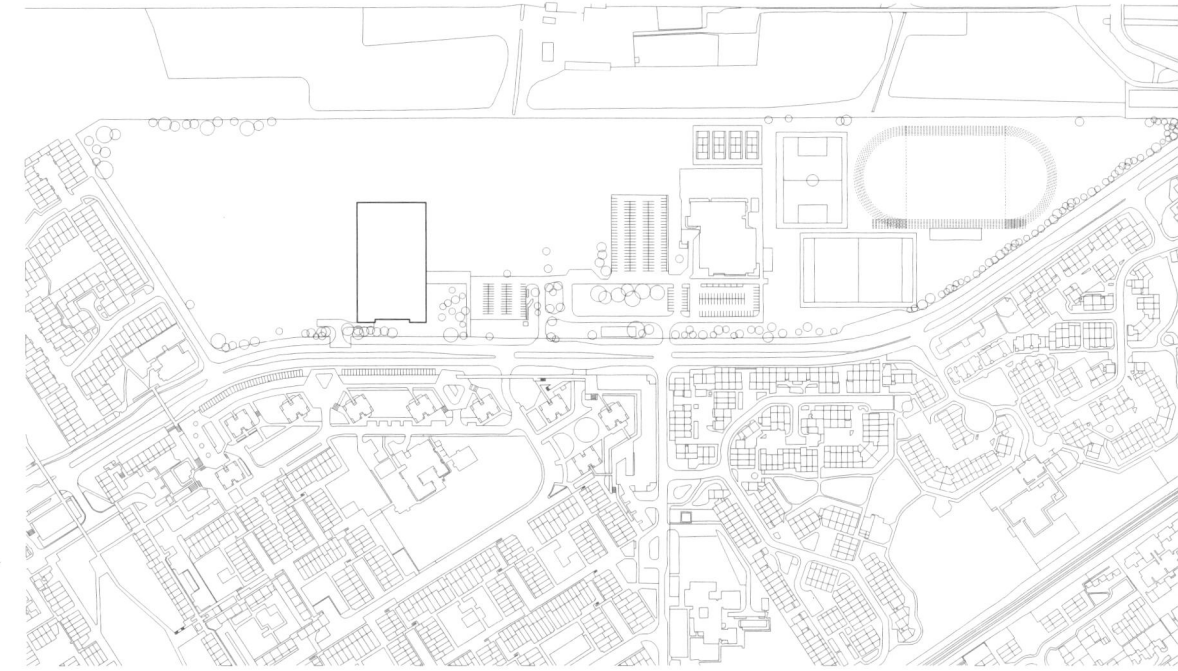

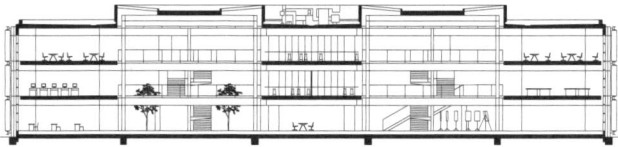

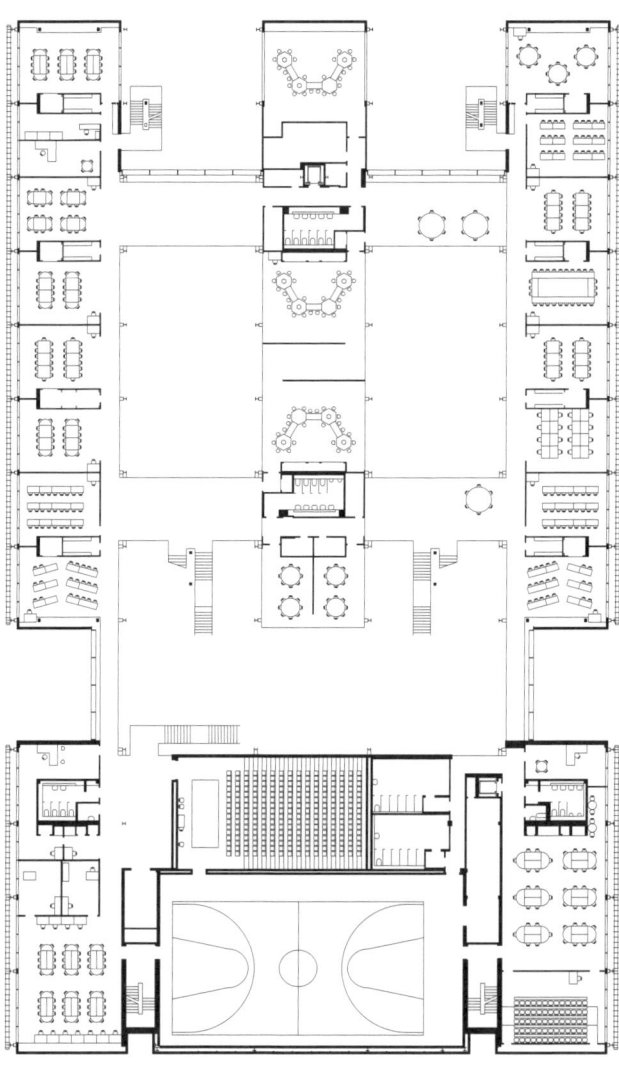

Anthology

After learning from so many different classrooms, and dwelling on them through the eyes and heads of many generations of teenagers, it is important to outline some prospective ambitions for this familiar-yet-unknown learning environment: it should be caring, resilient, emancipatory, independent, self-governed and free. And, to make further progress on this path, we need to listen to those who taught us so many of these choices, those fellow learners who planted these seeds in the minds of many learning collectives: that is, teachers. This very brief anthology is a place to give voice to those who work every day to make learning happen, allowing us to dwell on their thoughts and draw prospective lines of further learning with them. Even learning how to de-school society, as the pedagogue Ivan Illich proposed, requires learning subjects as well as learning actors, and someone who activates the network. Learning from each other will always require a network, and some other people to learn alongside.

The Boarding Schools in the Liberated Areas of the Guinean Territory

Half a century after the disappearance of Amílcar Cabral, Sónia Vaz Borges shines a light on the schools in the forest where the construction of a new nation was underway, happening simultaneously with the broader fight for liberation from colonial power. These secondary schools were practicing the same freedom that the nation was preparing for.

Sónia Vaz Borges, 2019

The creation of these boarding schools aimed to respond to the families' situation, in particular those children whose parents were at the war front or who were war orphans. The rules and diligence in the creation and location of a boarding school were similar to the ones for Tabanca Schools. According to the internal Party regulations, students who attended the boarding school would receive "the necessary preparation that later will allow them to attend other schools".

In the liberated areas of Guinea Bissau, PAIGC established three boarding schools with dorms. The first boarding school that opened in the territory was located in the north region of the country, in an area called Morés, from 1965 to 1966. Years later, for safety reasons, the school was transferred to the Sara region. Lassana Seidi, one of the first students of the boarding school, recalls the school's creation and its conditions:

The teacher, Anselmo Cabral, was *responsavél* for education and created the first school at Morés military base. The first professor was Paulo Cabral de Almada, the younger brother of Fidelis Cabral de Almada. Simultaneously, [the Party] ordered the surrounding villages to set up schools. For example, there was a village near the second military base, in the direction towards Mansoa, and there they created a school, with professor Adão Touré. When they created schools in the military base and the surrounding villages, those schools were the first PAIGC schools in the north.

[...] In that time, there were no tables. We were in the forest. You would search for trees, cut the branches, and some palm trees, and we would make tables out of them, in the clearings in the forest. The blackboard would be hung on a tree, and, in this way, the teacher would give the classes. In the beginning, there was no school material. When we were learning the A-B-C-D, a normal pencil was cut in two, sometimes even three, according to the numbers of students.[1]

Around the same period, the teacher Adelino Sousa Delgado created, in the south region of Guinea Bissau, the second Party boarding school. The name under which the boarding school came to be known—Aerolino Lopes Cruz boarding school—was a tribute to a teacher who, according to testimonies, lost his life during an air raid when taking his pupils to a bomb shelter. Following the same life rhythm and organization of the boarding school in Morés, the Aerolino Lopes Cruz boarding school stands out for its constant changing of location due to the constant Portuguese air raids of which it was victim. From its creation in 1965/66 to 1974, the school changed places ten times.

1. Interview with Lassana Seidi, June 3, 2014.

The Abel Djassi Military School,[2] located in the east region in Madina do Boé, was the third and last boarding school created by PAIGC. The school's directors, Segunda Lopes and Mario Cabral, founded it in 1969–1970. Segunda Lopes recalls her task as school director:

> The school had 275 students, all of whom were under my responsibility. But we had other teachers. […] I was in charge of getting the school materials in Conakry and bringing all the material to Lugajole, the place where the State of Guinea Bissau was proclaimed. The boarding school was located there too. The material was kept in the warehouse. In addition to teaching and coordinating the boarding school, I also cooked for all those kids and washed their clothes too. […] At that time we built tents to teach in, but we were always alert to the airplane noise. If you heard the sound of one, you would take all the kids to hide under the rocks. We stayed there, lying down, until the airplane disappeared. It was a weariness, a very great weariness. [3]

The regular maintenance of these boarding schools was always difficult for PAIGC. Security issues, high number of students, teacher and teaching capacities and conditions, lack of school supplies, but above all the inability to provide enough nourishment to students in these facilities were just some of the problems that the Party and the boarding schools' directors and regional *responsavéis* had to deal with on a daily basis. A meeting held in 1971 marked the closure of the East boarding school. In that meeting, there was an appeal to the *responsavéis* of each region to be realistic and responsible when considering whether to open a new school:

2. The name *Abel Djassi* was the pseudonym adopted by Amílcar Cabral in 1960.

3. Interview with Segunda Lopes, May 26, 2014.

189

We are willing to do all we can so that the boarding schools can do their work. But we have to be realistic. The boarding school is set up wherever it's possible, where there can be enough food for the boarding school. If that is not possible, comrades, it is better not to create a boarding school. [...] The Party can give clothes, all the work material, even some products like milk, but the Party cannot guarantee rice for boarding schools, there is no way to do so. And when there is no rice for the boarding schools, then we close them, even if we stay ignorant ten years longer [...]. Another issue that was raised was the closure of the eastern front boarding school. I knew that it was going to be closed down.[4]

The boarding schools
in the neighbouring countries
of Republic of Guinea
and Republic of Senegal

The Experimental School and the kindergarten Bellevue, both located in the Republic of Guinea, and the Teranga School, situated in the Republic of Senegal, were PAIGC's extraterritorial boarding schools. A result of Cassacá Congress, the idea was to create a boarding school that would set an example to all the PAIGC schools, and a space where experimental pedagogies and programmes would be developed, and where the future of Guinean education would be designed. Thus, the Experimental School was inaugurated on January 23, 1965.

It was founded with some of the youngsters present at the Cassacá Congress, along with some others who, for various reasons, were evacuated from the liberated areas. The first space where the school functioned was in Lar do Bonfim, a space that functioned as a hospital but also as a Party training centre, where militants would learn how to read and write and receive political training. The congress inspired enthusiasm, and the project was described by Luis Cabral as a "great reward, [to train the youth]

4. PAIGC, *Reunião do Conselho Superior da Luta*, 1971, pp. 5–6.

190

in order to form cadres that would better serve our Party and our people [...], forming young people who would become founders of our Experimental School [...], one specially designed for them".[5] Other testimonies revealed alternative reasons behind the school's creation:

> The school would receive those children who already had completed their first studies in the countryside, so that they could continue their studies and then travel abroad to do their technical and professional courses.[6]

Ana Maria Cabral's testimony, together with Luis Cabral's memories recalling life at the first school in Lar do Bonfim, speaks of "the girls who came with us (between 12 and 15 years old), who, apart from one or two of them, had never attended school. The alphabet was taught to them in our boarding school, and there were a few who learned to put together syllables and form words or sentences and read, even without understanding."[7] Thus, we can see that although the PAIGC initially set out to create a school for all ages, ultimately they focused on children and youths, with an age range between 12 and 17 years old.

The plan for an educational facility for younger age groups was still in process, and such was a result of Domingos Ramos' initiative and the support that PAIGC received from the Sekou Touré government who donated the space for the Experimental School facility. It was developed with the help of militants and foreign contributions, where future pupils played a significant role in the school's construction and cleaning, as some of them recalled: "I remember when PAIGC got the place for the Experimental School. Before all students were transferred to the school, we would go there and do volunteer work on Saturdays and Sundays. I was very young, but I remember very well the time that we went there to clean and organize the space. One day the school opened, and we were sent [to live] there."[8] Located in Ratoma neighbourhood, the school was initially a set

5. Cabral, Luis, *Crónica da libertação,* O Jornal: Lisbon, 1984, p. 187.

6. Interview with Ana Maria Cabral, September 5, 2013.

7. Cabral, Luis, *op. cit.,* p. 188.

8. Interview with Braima Sambu Auó, June 24, 2014.

191

of "shacks and a courtyard, and later the Party gradually extended it and built more shacks inside that space."[9] With improvements made, by the year of 1973, the school area had five classrooms, a kitchen and two canteens, a pharmacy and health centre, three dorms (one for girls, one for boys and one for female teachers), one storehouse, a sports field, a house garden and a pigsty.

The Teranga School[10] was the last boarding school created by the PAIGC. Inaugurated on January 12 1972, the school was located in Zinguinchor in the Republic of Senegal. Very little is known about the circumstances and the construction of this boarding school. The PAIGC's archives and militant testimonies did not have any information on how the Senegalese government allowed the construction of the school on its territory, or how much was spent on its construction. The scant information that it was possible to obtain includes that some of the resources to build the school came with the support of the Red Cross and the United Nations High Commissioner at the time, who was Algerian and a "friend" of the PAIGC liberation struggle.[11]

The initial school population was formed by students and teachers from liberated areas, in particular from the northern boarding school of Mores, and the semi-boarding school in Campada. The reason behind its construction was to alleviate the high flow of students to the Experimental School, which, by that time, had reached its limit. Therefore, the construction of the *Escola Teranga* was intended not only to reduce the number of students in the Experimental School, but also to help maintain the quality of teaching at the PAIGC schools and thus better prepare students for studying abroad. Marcelino Mutna, a student from the south area in Quitafene, recalls his trajectory to Teranga School, and the learning and living conditions there:

> I went to school in 1965, in the *tabanca* Tafore, in Quitafene. My first *tabanca* was near the Cacine river, and we could not stay there because we were constantly being bombed by the enemy boats that would come from the barracks in Cameconde.

9. Interview with Maria da Luz Boal, September 2, 2013.

10. The name "Teranga" is also written by some as "Terranga", but both refer to the same school. In Wolof, the language of the native Wolof people who are distributed along the territory of Senegal, Gambia and Mauritania, the word "teranga" means "friendship".

11. Interview with Maria da Luz Boal, September 2, 2013.

My first professor was Guilherme Pereira, then
Marciano Lima, and later Leonel Dioma. Those
three professors gave us classes until 1969. In 1968,
I finished the fourth grade, but there was no
professor for the fifth grade, so we continued to do
a class that they called 4A and 4B until they opened
the boarding school in Campon, which was in
another *tabanca*. […] We studied the fifth and the
sixth grade. With what the professor Felinto taught
us, sometimes me and Néné Njata and other
classmates would compete with the Inhabo high
school in Ziguinchor. They were in more advanced
classes, but we were in fact more advanced than
them because at our school we had excellent
materials to do experiments with oxygen and
hydrogen and other chemistry exercises.[12]

Vaz Borges, Sónia, "Building and Organizing Educational Structures in Guinea Bissau (1963–1972)," in *Militant Education, Liberation Struggle, Consciousness: The PAIGC education in Guinea Bissau 1963-1978*, Berlin: Peter Lang, 2019, pp. 78–92.

12. Interview with
Marcelino Mutna, June 5,
2014.

Path to School: Education, Architecture and Academic Exchanges

Anísio Teixeira fought for a school that would nurture and protect, that would expand education beyond instruction and literacy. The commitment of the architect Hélio Duarte, with his bold ideas, transformed the educational landscape in Brazil. Angelo Bucci charts this path to a more inclusive kind of school, and he denounces the assassination of its first traveller.

Angelo Bucci, 2017

The Educator
(Anísio Teixeira)

In 1971, the body of Brazil's greatest exponent of education was found at the bottom of a lift shaft in a Rio de Janeiro building, as if he had accidentally fallen inside. Anísio Teixeira would have turned seventy-one later that same year. As in an act of tragic theatre, this scene foreshadowed the dismantling of public education that would take place over the following years.

The circumstances surrounding the death of Teixeira are still awaiting clarification. The official version never coincided with the perception of his family and close friends. This fact would only come to light more widely and consistently in 2012, when the work of the National Truth Commission (CNV) opened. That year, on November 6, the detailed report, with eleven pages on the case of Teixeira, was forwarded to Gilson Dipp,

194

then-coordinator of the CNV, requesting an investigation.
The report—signed by Carlos Antonio Ferreira Teixeira (son of
Anísio Teixeira), Haroldo Borges Rodrigues Lima (his great-
nephew) and João Augusto de Lima Rocha (editor of the book
Anísio em Movimento, published in 1990 and reprinted by the
Senate in 2002)—reveals the chronology of the events that
occurred between March 11 (1971), the date of his disappearance,
and March 14, the date of his burial. This chronology highlights
several contradictions and inconsistencies in the official version.
In addition, it exhibits the press coverage, which, at the time,
already cast doubt on the hypothesis of an accident. The authors
of the report believe that Teixera might have been killed
following torture. They believe that the body would then have
been deposited in the lift shaft of the building on Avenida Rui
Barbosa, Botafogo, in order to cover up the crime. [...] The case
merited particular attention in the works and final publication of
the CNV [chapter 2, item F, pp. 79-80]. However, the results
could not be conclusive, given the lack of the post mortem
report, so the CNV requested the exhumation of the bodily
remains and their examination by the Institute of Legal
Medicine of the Federal District, which was not done until the
deadline for actions by the CNV, as stipulated in December 2014.
It is still not known exactly how Teixeira died.

Let us return to the life of the educator, which is the
subject here.

Born in Caetité, 500 kilometres west of Ilhéus, in Bahia,
Anísio Teixeira graduated in Law from the Federal University of
Rio de Janeiro. Soon after finishing his studies, in 1924, he
became Secretary (General Inspector) of Education for the State
of Bahia. In 1925, he travelled to Europe to learn about the
public education system in France, and he visited the United
States for the same reason in 1927. Two years later, in 1929, he
would return to America to graduate with a Master of Arts from
Columbia University, New York. During that period he met
John Dewey, the distinguished philosopher and professor at
Columbia, and, most likely through Dewey himself, he learned

about the public school system that was being forged in Detroit at the time, the so-called *platoon schools*. Indeed, the booming industry in 1920s Detroit placed the city right at the centre of the scene—in this case, it was a troubled scene, marked by conflicts along lines of class, race and ethnicity. The construction of an urban and public education system in Detroit was the result of struggles for the rights of workers, via the Detroit Labour Federation, and teachers, who had organised into the American Federation of Teachers. They fought against child labour and stood up for a quality education, considered emancipatory. They debated public spending on education, they discussed the suitable content and educational activities, they thought about the role of the institution, i.e. the school, in society. [...] That is, there was certain crossover between Dewey's philosophy and the birth of the urban public school system in Detroit. In any case, it was through Dewey that Teixeira got to know the education system, and this would shape the rest of his life's work.

Why and how did Detroit's schools impact Teixeira so much? Essentially, because of the strength of the synthesis that they represented. The main achievement of that historic experience was undoubtedly the synthesis achieved, to the extent that it was possible to understand it via a diagram, even before any building, and independent of it. I am referring to the diagram that clearly demonstrates how the proposed system responded very well—in addition to the teaching goals—to the economic and efficiency demands, which were such crucial issues in that industrial city. The strength of this strategy lies in its extreme simplicity: the children are divided into two identically-sized groups, and they alternate in the spaces, in order to optimise the use of the built structure: in other words, the occupation is doubled. It should be noted that there are two groups of students, for two groups of projected spaces that correspond to two groups of complementary activities. [...] The arrangement of shifts, or schedules, is perfectly consistent with this same scheme. This is, in fact, its great advantage: the groups alternate in different periods, in the same spaces. It is precisely because they are organised into groups that the name *platoon* was consecrated—it is an insufficient name for such an elaboration. In fact, it is an unfortunate term even in its military sense, and it ended up giving its critics a simple image: regiments of pupils as platoons of poor workers' children. This was the negative image that critics of the model would use to camouflage their true motivation: to stoke class conflict [...].

Evidently, Teixeira did not align with those criticisms. Instead, he clung to the potential that he saw in that system, using it as inspiration for his own responses to be applied to the Brazilian context. Indeed, he would dedicate himself to this endeavour until the end of his life.

Teixeira's relationship with Columbia University had not been casual or episodic. Although John Dewey's pragmatism had had a great impact on his education, Teixeira's own work did not go unnoticed by the institution. So much so that, in 1963, he would receive the Honour Medal from Columbia University, and the following year, after being removed as rector of the University of Brasília, he would teach as a visiting professor at Columbia.

The Architect
(Hélio Duarte)

In 1973, still impacted by the shock of Anísio Teixeira's death, and under the overbearing weight of that same political context, Hélio Duarte published *Escolas Classe - Escola Parque*.

[...] Hélio Duarte (Rio de Janeiro, 1906) graduated from the School of Fine Arts in Rio in 1930. In 1935, he moved to Salvador, Bahia, before moving to São Paulo in 1944. Although his geographical journey across Brazil was almost the opposite of that of Teixeira, they would meet.

Duarte was already in São Paulo when, along with Diógenes Rebouças, he designed the project for the Popular Education Centre (Carneiro Ribeiro School) that opened in 1950 in Salvador de Bahia. At that point, since the end of 1948, the School Agreement between the Municipality and State of

197

São Paulo had already been signed. Duarte had a brief but decisive role in the Agreement, which was created to design the network of schools and related equipment. It was precisely in the foundation of the Agreement that the Department of Buildings (EDIF) of the City of São Paulo (which took on that initial scope, i.e. the school network and its related equipment) would soon expand to health buildings and other public buildings. In addition, the School Agreement coincides, both in time and in many of its actors—such as Eduardo Corona, Roberto Tibau, Oswaldo Corrêa Gonçalves and Ernest Robert de Carvalho Mange—with the foundation, in 1949, of the School of Architecture of the University of São Paulo (FAUUSP).

Within São Paulo's architectural scene, one gets the impression that everything was defined in that period of time (1948-1952), or, more broadly, between 1943, when the Institute of Brazilian Architects (IAB) was founded, and 1954, marked by the opening of Ibirapuera Park, which was a milestone. Duarte participated as co-author of the IAB headquarters project.

For almost five years, a period in which he was in the School Agreement until he left in 1952, Duarte signed several projects. It was during this same period that he delved deeper into the concepts of education, always guided by Teixeira, whom he simply called Dr Rieux (in an allusion to the character-narrator of Albert Camus's novel *The Plague*). Duarte's projects paid close attention and remained faithful to the principles that Teixeira had brought in and elaborated from the platoon schools. Duarte eventually compiled them in *Escolas Classe - Escola Parque*; its collection of educational projects is remarkable, ranging from school groups to university campuses [...].

In any case, Duarte had withdrawn from the Agreement in 1952. It is possible that he already harboured some frustrations with it, related to the gap between what was foreseen in the project and what actually took place in that particular economic, political and administrative context.

[...] In 1973, when he was dedicated exclusively to FAUUSP, he wrote *Escolas Classe – Escola Parque*, a text that marked the culmination of his career as an architect-teacher. It was written in honour of Teixeira, and in this seminal book the educator's thought takes an extraordinary importance and a special meaning for the realm of architectural thought. Duarte does something remarkable: he demonstrates Teixeira's thoughts and strategies through diagrams, and the scheme of Detroit's public schools, as witnessed by Teixeira, is thus made visible to everyone. Duarte undoubtedly achieved his two goals for that publication: to pay homage to Teixeira, and mainly to bring the educator's ideas closer to architectural thinking. The text provides a clear glimpse of how Teixeira, with the great ambition of a generous and modest man, solves his most ambitious equation: he sought to pave the way for an educational system in Brazil that would guarantee "accessible quality education for all". The precedent set by the platoon schools in Detroit was indeed crucial for him: by dividing students into two groups, it became possible to superimpose two simultaneous schools in parallel. Firstly, there would be one school that "instructed" through the triad of *reading, writing, and arithmetic* (known as the "three R's"), with a teacher in each room, the *homeroom*. Teixeira would refer to this as *escolas classe*. The second, meanwhile, educated the children via a programme of activities in literature, geography, art, music, manual work, domestic sciences, theatre and physical activities; this was an *enriched programme*, with several specific teachers for each subject or activity. Teixeira would call this second one *escola parque*. The two would combine in such a way that every four *escolas classe* would correspond to one *escola parque*, with capacity for the total set of students from the four *escolas classe*. By alternating morning and afternoon shifts, all spaces would be in use throughout the day, in order to maximise the use of the public facilities. Arithmetically designed from the ideal number of students per class-room—500 students per class—four *escolas classe* would be combined with one *escola parque*, the latter with the capacity for 2,000 students. A systemic view.

199

In the concluding paragraphs of the book there is a certain tone of disenchantment, although this was not the message the author wanted to convey. On the contrary: he strives to end with a message of hope, but even so, he fails to soften his flagrant dismay [...].

Duarte led a fruitful life, so the fact that he had a prevailing sense of frustration and dismay is very sad. This lingered in such a way that, in a 1985 interview, when he was asked about the result of schools as neighbourhood nuclei, he replied with a single word: "nothing".

We would be right back at the bottom of the lift shaft.

The Duality
(which they both represent)

But there is another route—and that's the main reason for this text.

There are no words to describe the brutality against Teixeira, whatever the outcome of the work to shed light on the circumstances of his death. I say this as a caveat to what follows below; the aim is only to look for another possible path, not to mitigate the implications of a possible crime. After all, I want to believe that his life was not all contained in that dead body. A man's work is a legacy that embodies a piece of his existence. Therefore, it would be possible to redo—and by redoing, it updates itself—the formulation of his long-awaited *Escolas Classe – Escola Parque*, based on a simple diagram recorded by Duarte. Such a diagram has condensed lives since the Detroit workers' struggle. It would not be possible, or it would be much more difficult, without Duarte's precious work.

From this account, we can see that Teixeira and Duarte acted as a duo, as if they were working side by side. From the perspective of FAUUSP, it is almost possible to confuse them, since they merge into a very special type of unit that only exists in the vibrant and complementary coexistence of two inseparable components: duality. This is a founding concept for architecture, present even in its very name. That is, two fields of knowledge—human and natural sciences—merge into a single word, to name and enable the activity of designing and building the world where human activities take place. And different actors engage in this duality, according to the relevance in each historical context: art and technique, theory and practice, form and function, matter and image, and so on. In the case of our two protagonists, the educator embodies the method—to use a duality evoked by Teixeira himself when, talking about John Dewey, he discusses how we learn—while the architect embodies the matter. The former, as an idea, holds the power of being open to several possible materialisations, while the latter, as a fact, has the beauty of crystallising ideas or life itself into what is built. Teixeira handles collectively matured principles, and he thus tends to be accepted as given without his ideas having to be adapted to suit each new circumstance; therefore, in his case, the notion of authorship normally has no relevance. Duarte's view requires a careful consideration of the context and circumstances so that it can be realised, and authorship is an important notion for two aspects, i.e. intrinsic responsibilities and to give the matter a properly human feature. Attention: one does not exist without the other.

Why/How to Build School Buildings

Giancarlo De Carlo raises an even more provocative question than the "who?" of his architecture of participation: here, he asks "why" we should build schools before discussing learning itself, and how/where it happens. This is a joyous anarchist jolt on notions of type, order, authorship and quality, with much to learn from.

Giancarlo De Carlo, 1969

In a period of crisis of values like the one which we are going through at present, we cannot deal with problems of "how to" without first posing the problems of "why." If we were to begin discussing immediately the best way to build school buildings for contemporary society without first clarifying the reasons for which contemporary society needs school buildings, we would run the risk of taking for granted definitions and judgments which may not make sense anymore; and our speculations would turn out to be sand castles.

We will begin, therefore, with four elementary questions, well aware that often the most elementary questions—which no one has posed for a long time because they seem so obvious—can help us to discover the hidden thread in the evolution of a new reality.

W.1

The first question:
"Is it really necessary for contemporary society that educational activity be organized in a stable and codified institution?"

W.2

The second question:
"Must educational activity take place in buildings designed especially for that purpose?"

W.3

The third question:
"Is there a direct and reciprocal relationship between educational activity and the quality of the buildings in which it goes on?"

W.4

The fourth question:
"Must the planning and construction of buildings for educational activity be entrusted to specialists?"

The fourth question leads into problems of "how," but at the same time it is connected to the first question on "why." In fact, it could be formulated more exactly in this way: "Must the planning and construction of a school building be entrusted to specialists trained by means of an institutional education which has specialized them in such a way that they consider fundamental the requirements of the institution?"

The four questions are therefore four points of a circular relationship which can be interrupted or continued at any point. We will examine them one at a time, looking for the most reasonable crossover points into the problems of "how."

A.1

Education is the result of experience. The wider and more complex the experience, the deeper and more intense the education. The field of experience widens in direct relation to the frequency *of contacts*, and its complexity grows with the *increase in their variety*.

Ideally, to ensure a really profound and intense education, no kind of experience should be denied: all possible contacts of whatever nature should be not only permitted but encouraged.

But institutions are organizational structures constituted for the attainment of pre-established goals: they cannot permit and encourage all kinds of experiences because they can permit and encourage only those experiences which serve the attainment of their goals.

Institutions limit both contacts and education. They institutionalize education so that it will be useful to the institutions, first for their consolidation, then for their defence.

During periods of expansion, societies had no need to organize educational activity. The problem arose only when the societies began to generate institutions, that is, when they passed from the stage of self-definition to the stage of accumulation and preservation. At this point education ceased to be coterminous with the entire field of experience of the society and became limited to the field of experiences permitted by the institutions.

[…] The student revolt which is flaring up all over the world at every level of education, and which has begun to infiltrate the professions as well, reveals a radical refusal of the condition of exclusion caused by an aprioristic, codified limitation of the field of cultural action. Perhaps specialization is indispensable, but the opinion is growing increasingly strong that it is acceptable only when the specialist has first achieved a broader understanding so that he is capable of maintaining the capacity to criticize—to accept, reject, or somehow choose, with a political consciousness of his action—the role which the individual assumes in the social context. The equation, "specialization = participation," is replacing the equation, "specialization = estrangement," implying the revolutionary overthrow of the whole existing institutional system and, in particular, the revolutionary overthrow of educational institutions.

With the student revolt, education has returned to the city and to the streets and has, thus, found a field of rich and diversified experience which is much more formative than that offered by the old school system. Perhaps we are headed toward an era in which education and total experience will again coincide, in which the school as an established and codified institution no longer has any reason for existence.

A.2

Education has always been conceived as a segregated activity. Plato taught while walking back and forth in the grove of Academe, and Aristotle in the enclosure of Apollo Lyceum, but these were cases, [...] of education which was not yet organized. When education began to become an institution, buildings were immediately made for the purpose of containing it and at the same time, isolating it from contacts with the surrounding environment. [...] Since the end of the nineteenth century, as the principle of specialization has consolidated itself, the subjects of specialization have multiplied and, with them, the types of scholastic building. Each branch of learning has had its type of building, specifically designed for its use and more or less differentiated from an organizational and structural point of view.

But in spite of the precise differences of definition and the vague differences of configuration, all these types have one feature in common: the strictest adherence to the principle of segregation. The school is a physical structure designed exclusively for education, for teachers and for students, just as a prison is a physical structure designed exclusively for imprisonment, for jailors and for prisoners; its function is to house a specific activity but also to isolate it from other activities.

[...] We know that, with time, this model has undergone a series of deformations. The expansion of mass education has

205

caused a wrench which has continued to alter the bars of the cage without changing, however, its nature as a cage. In certain cases the spaces between the bars have actually widened—for example, in the case of elementary and professional education—when the necessity for a greater diffusion of centres of learning has made it necessary to mix them in with the fabric of the city. But the cage has continued to be a cage: the school building has continued to be a very distinct and autonomous physical structure, a point which sticks out, breaking the continuity of the fabric in which it finds itself [...].

To the inevitable observation that these authoritarian and monumental characteristics are more typical of 19th century schools than of present ones, we can reply that a series of classrooms served by a corridor is substantially equivalent to a series of classrooms served by a common space and that the monumentalness of the columns and decorations in cement is substantially equivalent to that of the steel framework and curtain wall. In architecture, in fact, organizational structures can be defined as authoritarian when the articulation of the spaces does not stimulate the community to exchange communications at any moment and at a level of complete equality. The formal configurations are considered monumental when they adapt themselves to the aesthetic codes of the institutions and are not receptive to the users' free expression [...].

School buildings built especially to house educational activity can house, therefore, only that part of this activity which is in the interest of the institutions which construct the school buildings. The rest of education—the richest and most active part—goes on elsewhere and has no need of buildings; or perhaps it has not yet found the appropriate spaces in which it could take place as a whole, becoming a part of a sphere of total experiences.

A.3

Socrates taught in the gymnasiums of Athens, and many centuries later Johann Heinrich Pestalozzi began his activity as an educator in a farm building at Neuhof near Zurich. Besides these two exemplary cases, there are many others in the history of education which show that a school can be excellent even though it is housed in an inappropriate, or even ugly, building. On the contrary, there are many cases of buildings considered excellent which house schools of very poor quality. We can be certain, then, that there is no direct and reciprocal relationship between architectural quality and the quality of the educational system. Architecture, because of its superstructural nature, can modify the environment directly; but it cannot dictate the activities that go on in the environment.

We know, however, that architecture, by acting on the environment, can exert influences on activities, orient or deviate their ways of coming about in the network of the complicated interplay of feedback through which form establishes a dynamic relationship with society.

[…] But what is order in a formal configuration, if not the expulsion of every expression which is inconsistent with the requirements of representation of the institutions? And what is this expulsion, if not a repressive act with regard to collective participation, an act which corresponds perfectly with the repression which the same institutions carry out in the political and social sphere? The correspondence is particularly evident in the school buildings where the principle of formal order which governs the architectural composition mirrors the principle of disciplinary order which is given as the definition of the purpose of educational activity. Contemporary school buildings—both those considered poor in quality and those considered excellent—do not escape this law of symmetry which mirrors the disciplinary order in the formal order. […] And this compositional structure mirrors the authoritarian procedure of educating an elite to exert cultural control over the whole society in the name of a particular social class to which the elite itself belongs. Authoritarianism and the aesthetics of order are correlated products of the rule of the class in power.

[…] Even though authoritarianism is still the mainstay of educational activity, it is clear by now that teaching cannot go on being authoritarian for very long. Likewise, it can be said that, even though the ideology of order is still the mainstay of the aesthetic code which governs scholastic architecture, it is clear by now that the architectural values of the future will be organized on the basis of a radical re-evaluation of disorder.

The very sound of the word "disorder" generally provokes uncontrollable nervousness. Therefore, it must be explained that disorder does not mean accumulations of systematic malfunctioning but, on the contrary, the expression of a higher type of functionality, capable of taking in and manifesting the complex interplay of all the variables involved in a spatial event. Order comes from a selection which isolates the variables considered significant and organizes them in a system which is as simple as possible, i.e., so as to offer a stable solution. We know that there is an increasing tendency toward the organization of physical space according to this reductive principle, and we know that it is the origin of all the methods based on addition which are universally applied to the construction of the environment; for example, the method based on the search for a typological order according to which it is possible to separate and attribute spatial prototypes—or a series of prototypes—to them. The combination by addition of these gives rise to an environmental whole: the street, the neighbourhood, the city. We also know that a city, a neighbourhood, or a street, even a building, is interesting to us exactly for all that which manages to escape from the controls of these rules, for the expressions which are "not permitted" but which insinuate themselves through cracks in the order and reveal themselves with all the wealth of stimuli which is the property of contradictions.

[…] To return to school buildings and to the problem of their qualitative turning point, we can conclude that the only possible way for them to exert a positive influence on educational activity is to revolutionize the procedure according to which they are planned and constructed. The school should not be an island but part of the physical context, or more precisely, the physical context as a whole, conceived as a function of the requirements of education. It should not be a closed apparatus but a structure spread out in the network of social activities, capable of articulating itself to their continual variations. It should not be an object represented according to the rules of an aprioristic aesthetic code, but an unstable configuration continually recreated by the direct participation of the collectivity that uses it, introducing into it the disorder of its unforeseeable expressions.

A.4

Collective participation in the formation of the environment implies radical changes in the role of the architect. If it is agreed that all expressions should be permitted, even if they give rise to situations of disorder; if it is established that these situations of disorder are legitimate, even though they are in contrast with the official aesthetic code based on the ideology of order; if to this disorder is attributed an inner logic which has not yet been revealed, only because it is complex and, therefore, beyond the elementary schemes which we are used to manipulating; if it is accepted that the impulses which bring about the definition of an environmental configuration should link themselves together freely in a process which generates solutions in continual renewal; if all this is considered consistent with the most progressive tendencies of society and, therefore, desirable; then the function of the architect must change in the same way that the functions of all the specialists operating in the different professional fields must change.

[...] In a situation of collective participation, the consideration of the network of interrelations which are established between every new project and the context to which it is destined becomes fundamental. To design a school building in this situation means to design a piece of the city, to enter into the city with a project which will be homogeneous, to change

209

the city to make it homogeneous with the project which is being designed, to act upon the whole field of urban forces and put it all into movement, foreseeing the consequences of this movement.

And finally the methodology of action is in question. The architect—more than any other professional—plans circumscribed and finished objects. His specific task is a function which he receives extracted from its context; he plans a structure suitable to its realization, within the limits of isolation from context, and shapes this structure into a physical form which represents the full context, giving it expression in physical space. But the procedure suffers at every stage from the abstractness accepted at the beginning when the activity was taken out of its context, cutting its ties with reality. The initial authoritarian decision reflects its burden of authoritarianism on the succeeding stages, which become in their turn authoritarian. The structures act as exclusive organizational systems; and the physical forms shape themselves as finished, inflexible representations, presumed to be that much nearer to aesthetic perfection the less space they leave for the accidental character of time and use.

[…] In a situation of collective participation, the organizational systems are necessarily included and inclusive as parts of a more general system which makes the whole of the activities indivisible. On the other hand, the forms must necessarily be open, which means defined only in the essential elements which generate and regulate their evolutionary process.

To design a school building for a situation of collective participation does not mean to lay down a succession of spaces connected by a single line of communication but rather to organize a place for opportunities for experience and to represent it in the physical space by means of a system of forms already oriented to the reception of the multiple and variable lines of expression of those who have the experiences.

De Carlo, Giancarlo, "Why/How to Build School Buildings,"
Harvard Educational Review, vol. 39, no. 4, Cambridge (Mass.), 1969, pp. 12–35.

Weaving a Tapestry of Resistance

Sharon Sutton weaves many forms of pedagogy and change into a delicate tapestry of resistance. Weaving—a traditional practice that builds the symbolic limits of intimacy in architecture—is transposed as a form of education, of togetherness, of the mutual reinforcement of differences. Diverse strands of a more resilient fabric.

Sharon E. Sutton

When Moses led the Jews out of Egypt, he and his followers spent forty years in the desert. The modern Israelis have proven in a number of recent wars that the Sinai is easily crossed, and even for the primitive transport of Moses's time, forty years of travel seems outlandish. Why did Moses and his followers take so long to cross this modest desert? It seems that the personal and social transitions from the fleshpots of Egypt to freedom in the Promised Land required a change of perceptions, and the human mind is not easily transformed. It was essential to give up the slave-like ways that had been learned in Egypt. By the time the Jews reached their homeland, all but two persons who remembered Egypt had died off, so that the new people, readied in the desert for the Promised Land, completed the journey and entered upon their inheritance reborn.[1]

1. Duhl, Leonard J., *The Social Entrepreneurship of Change*, New York: Pace University Press, 1990.

211

If places are texts that instruct children about a way of life, what types of landscapes might enable them to take leave of their assigned ranks and roles in the hierarchies of the dominant culture? Lacking a period of isolation such as Moses had to relinquish the atomistic, authoritarian belief systems upon which most of our careers are built, how can educators adopt more inclusive, participatory instructional methods? Given the concentration of wealth and power in the hands of a few persons—given the extraordinary calcification of the social order—what processes might give us the inner strength and will to start a movement to reconceive Earthly relationships? These three questions outline one dimension of a model of learning in a sustainable society, encompassing physical contexts, governance structures, and learning processes. They form the warp of what I refer to as a *tapestry of resistance* to the status quo; they are the continuous threads that are the foundation of the mental shift I am about to describe. The other dimension relates to how revolutionary individuals choose to be in transforming those three aspects of mainstream education.

In the introduction, I discussed the urgent need for redefining traditional approaches to education due to the population explosion and its accompanying depletion of the landscape worldwide. As a number of persons in the environmental movement have noted, two Chinese characters translate into the word *crisis,* the first meaning "danger," the second meaning "opportunity." What many perceive as profound threats to the future of life on the planet also create unique occasions for personal and social growth. While it seems inconceivable that those few persons who exercise power over the Earth's resources (including the very conception of human potential) would voluntarily surrender such power, perhaps it is possible. Until now in modern Western society, members of the dominant culture have thought of themselves as autonomous beings, the best and the brightest of whom move into positions of power within the institutions that make up the larger society. As it becomes increasingly clear that no one exists in isolation—that our fates are linked through the ecosystem—the haves might be convinced to share their power and join with the have-nots in collective resistance to enslaving patriarchal contracts. Perhaps it *is* possible.

Within sustainable relationships, power would be experienced not as a negative force but as a positive one—sometimes referred to as *empowerment*—that results in feelings of mutual responsibility and personal control. Henry Giroux commented on Paulo Freire's notions of power as both a negative and positive force.

> For Freire, power works both on and through people. On the one hand, this means that domination is never so complete that power is experienced exclusively as a negative force. On the other hand, it means that power is at the basis of all forms of behaviour in which people resist, struggle, and fight for their image of a better world.[2]

This view of power as a positive, empowering struggle for equity is generally invoked with respect to disadvantaged persons who are seeking to increase their fair share of resources. I have attempted to show that the struggle for a better world must also take place among privileged groups who are setting the norms for unsustainable lifestyles by imposing on impoverished persons "their way of being, talking, dancing, their tastes, even their way of eating".[3] The concept of empowerment necessarily includes those affluent persons who must gain the courage to share their advantages.

But what would a tapestry of collective resistance look like? If education in a sustainable society is about inclusiveness, how can persons with diverse political views participate in differing, but complementary, ways. bell hooks recalled the intensity of her early education in a segregated southern school in which black "teachers were enacting a revolutionary pedagogy of resistance that was profoundly anticolonial"[4] by teaching black children that they could be reborn as scholars and thinkers.

2. Giroux, Henry A., "Introduction", in Freire, Paulo, *The Politics of Education: Culture, Power and Liberation*, Westport (CT): Bergin and Garvey, 1985, p. xix.

3. Freire, Paulo, *op. cit.*, p. 192.

4. hooks, bell, *Teaching to Transgress: Education as the Practice of Freedom*, New York: Routledge, 1994, p. 2.

She contrasted that experience with attending imprisoning integrated schools in which white teachers reinforced racial stereotypes—places in which apathy, boredom, and disinterest replaced the joyous struggle for personal and social growth that hooks had known in her all-black school. What kind of pedagogies would create places of resistance—Promised Lands—in which teachers and students of all socioeconomic backgrounds could struggle to be reborn as members of a heterogeneous and sustainable society? I use the plural deliberately to avoid the shortsightedness of proposing a single conceptual framework, and because I believe that there is a continuum of possibilities for engaging in resistance, depending on how individuals see themselves in relation to the mainstream. This continuum of possibilities forms the second dimension of the tapestry, or its woof—the varied threads that loop around the warp, bringing colour, life, and multiple dimensions to it.

[…] Among the ranks of conventional change agents are those educators who seek to broaden students' understanding of social issues through community-service learning, a pedagogy described earlier that has a long-standing tradition in elementary, secondary, and higher education. More recent are those involved in diversifying curricula to include multicultural or feminist perspectives. In these instances, the larger institution does not change, but individual educators create alternative learning spaces for their students.

The most transformative threads in the tapestry are educators like Myles Horton, who believed that the school system had become too corrupted by its own power to ever promote real social change. As Horton did, such persons leave the mainstream and find other venues for engaging in out-of-school education, but this may result in a loss of one's status and recognition.

[…] Another progressive educator, Paulo Freire, shared Horton's commitment to liberatory education for oppressed persons but chose to work within the system, thus falling somewhere in the centre of this continuum of possibilities. Freire accepted that the school system was intractable but felt it was important to create change-making subcultures within mainstream institutions. Hooks and others have written about the duality of being inside an institution while struggling against its norms, referring to this position as one of creative marginality. Marginality is "a site one stays in, clings to even, because it nourishes one's capacity to resist. It offers to one the possibility of radical perspective from which to see and create, to imagine alternatives, new worlds".[5] These three points along the continuum—which I refer to respectively as conventional, transformative, and alternative—seem equally valuable and necessary to widespread personal and social change. [...] To give this idealized model a real-world grounding, I illustrate its varied possibilities for resistance to the status quo—its woof—with concrete examples. These include a program that created an innovative environment within a traditional school ("Threads of a Conventional Woof"), another that changed traditional operational procedures ("Threads of an Alternative Woof"), and a third that created a community-based context of learning ("Threads of a Transformative Woof") [...].

Education as the Practice of Weaving

Weaving—the metaphor for the educational approach presented in this book—"makes use of many different threads to create something larger, stronger, more useful, more durable, and more beautiful than any individual string".[6] Through weaving, educators can create a tapestry of human connectedness, where more and less gifted, young and old, poor and privileged can use the inspiration of cultural activity to bridge their differences; where children and adults feel empowered by a process of defining a strong, collective purpose; where a community of people take responsibility for guiding change and for bettering the human condition in a way that respects the sacredness of nature. Teaching as the practice of weaving means that educators would venture beyond nurturing intellectual life to assume a broader socializing function —it means that they would trade in

5. hooks, bell, *Yearning: Race, Gender, and Cultural Politics*, Boston: South End Press, 1990, p. 150.

6. Tainter, S., "Weaving the Urban Network", *The University of Michigan Research News*, January/February 1990, p. 2.

215

their stance of objectivity and openly assume responsibility for shaping the nation's consciousness. By accepting the position of being unbiased, apolitical technocrats, educators are disempowered from intervening in those ideas that give meaning and purpose to a society, relegated instead to providing the state with a literate population that speaks a common language and shares a middle-class ethic of delayed gratification.

[...] Yet, those who develop literacy are major contributors to the moral foundation of a society because language is a filter of what we know and do (with direct experience and belief systems being the other filters). Environmental lessons are being taught every day through countless words and actions, so the issue is how to make these lessons socially responsible. It is how to educate citizens who can actively engage in an ongoing process of articulating the common concerns of this diverse planet—of elaborating a philosophy-in-action that can transform how we see ourselves. Active participation at both the personal and societal levels is especially important at this moment in history because open dialogue is necessary for deriving collective responses to current environmental challenges. In the words of Frances Moore Lappé:

> A democratic society is more than a collection of people developing their individual talents and shouldering responsibility. It is also the dynamic of the common life itself, in which citizenship means joining in public dialogue to uncover and give shape to our common values and to decide how to act upon them. Citizenship [...] promotes a public arena of deliberation over common concerns, an interchange that is itself morally transformative, inseparable from our individual moral development.[7]

7. Lappé, Frances Moore and Du Bois, Paul Martin, *The Quickening of America: Community-households in Harlem*, New York: Columbia University Press, 1994, p. 63.

To assure the survival of life on Earth in the twenty-first century, substantive discussions are needed in every arena —in classrooms as well as on the streets of neighbourhoods, in the workplace as

216

well as around kitchen tables, in the media as well as in local organizations, in religious as well as political arenas, in art galleries as well as gift shops. Since educators knowingly or unknowingly transmit the values that will shape future ecosystems, it seems entirely appropriate for them *to* assume a leadership role in articulating more inclusive, equitable values and norms. [...] The question is not *whether* educators should expand their institutional obligations to encompass a social justice agenda; rather it is *how to begin* an integrated agenda to personal and social growth within a context of environmental sustainability.

Giroux, Henry A. and Freire, Paulo (eds.), *Weaving a Tapestry of Resistance*, Westport (CT): Praeger, 1996, pp. 197–200 and 220–222.

Acknowledgements

Joaquim Moreno expresses a deeply felt gratitude for the kindness, generosity and intelligence of all the fellow travellers in this major learning endeavour: Andy Hinchliff, Éric Varnier, Christian Gröne, Carlos Marques, Anne Auclair, Julia Albani, Max Risselada, Roy Kozlovsky, Maristella Casciato, Jean-Louis Cohen, Urtzi Grau, Jorge Carvalho, Emanuel Pacheco, Susana Camanho, Emídio Agra, Nicolas Stutzin, Carol Tonetti, Angelo Bucci, Vanessa Grossman, Alejandra Celedón, Ahmed Belkhodja, Graça Campolargo, Maria Mendes, Tom Holert, Wenwen Cai, Leonardo Lella, Eva Franch, Francesca Hughes, Maria Moita, Dan Ferrand-Bechmann, Nivaldo Júnior, Ariadne Moraes, Paulo Pires do Vale, Hannah Strothmann, Daniella Figueiredo, Rita Brito, Isabel Clemente, Margarida Cruz, Maria Cunha, Teresa Cunha, Rafael Jesus, Camila Maia, Maria Miranda Melo, Maria Mourinha, Anita Peixoto, Catarina Pereira, João Pires, Beatriz Rego, Tomás Sá, Ana Saraiva, João Viegas, Francisco Vinagre, Anna Beda and the CRS Center at Texas A&M University School of Architecture, the archives of FAUFBA (Architecture School of Bahia's Federal University) and the AA Library and its students.

Co-funded by
the European Union

CCB

With the support of

  FUNDAÇÃO **MILLENNIUM BCP** **OTIIMA** Much more than a window.

arc en rêve
centre
d'architecture

With the support of

SAISON TEMPORADA FRANCE PORTUGAL PORTUGAL FRANÇA 2022   RÉPUBLIQUE FRANÇAISE Liberté Égalité Fraternité   REPÚBLICA PORTUGUESA   CAMÕES INSTITUTO DA COOPERAÇÃO E DA LÍNGUA PORTUGAL MINISTÉRIO DOS NEGÓCIOS ESTRANGEIROS   GEPAC GABINETE DE ESTRATÉGIA, PLANEAMENTO E AVALIAÇÃO CULTURAIS   INSTITUT FRANÇAIS

Ville de **BORDEAUX**   PRÉFET DE LA RÉGION NOUVELLE-AQUITAINE Liberté Égalité Fraternité   RÉGION Nouvelle-Aquitaine   **BORDEAUX MÉTROPOLE**   Gironde LE DÉPARTEMENT   ACADÉMIE DE BORDEAUX Liberté Égalité Fraternité

z33

With the support of

 **Flanders** State of the Art

Exhibition co-produced by
Centro Cultural de Belém / Garagem Sul Architecture Centre (Lisbon, Portugal)
arc en rêve centre d'architecture (Bordeaux, France)
Z33 House for Contemporary Art, Design and Architecture (Hasselt, Belgium)

Represented by
André Tavares (Architecture Programmer CCB)
Fabrizio Gallanti (Director arc en rêve)
Adinda Van Geystelen (Director Z33)

Curator
Joaquim Moreno

Assistant curator
Ivo Poças Martins

Graphic design
Studio Thomas Spallek

Partnership CCB
Plano Nacional das Artes

Advisory board Z33
Loïc de Béthune and Maarten Van Den Driessche (Ghent University)

Exhibition design
FURO (CCB)
Cyrille Brisou and Denys Zhdanov (arc en rêve)
Pauline Clarot and Leander Venlet (Z33)

Films
Luís Leitão and Aurélio Vasques

Drawings
Bruno Pinto da Cruz

Project coordination
Margarida Ventosa (CCB)
Wenwen Cai and Leonardo Lella (arc en rêve)
Geert Driessen (Z33)

Press and communication
Sofia Cardim and Sofia Mântua (CCB)
Christophe Catsaros (arc en rêve)
Veerle Ausloos and Mariam Nazaryan (Z33)

Translation and proofreading of the exhibition texts
Justin Jaeckle, João Moço and Pedro Morais (CCB)
Jean-Marc Agostini and Martyn Back (arc en rêve)
Marthy Locht and Mattie Wolters (Z33)

Education and mediation
Inês Marques and Sofia Passadouro (CCB)
Sara Meunier and Flora Stich (arc en rêve)
Kiki Goossen and Willem Vrancken (Z33)

Exhibition views
Selma Gurbuz (Z33)
Tiago Casanova (CCB)
Marion Parent (arc en rêve)

Focus teen group CCB
Daniella Figueiredo (mediation), Rita Brito (content editor), Isabel Clemente, Margarida Cruz, Maria Cunha, Teresa Cunha, Rafael Jesus, Camila Maia, Maria Miranda Melo, Maria Mourinha, Anita Peixoto, Catarina Pereira, João Pires, Beatriz Rego, Tomás Sá, Ana Saraiva, João Viegas, Francisco Vinagre

Exhibition set-up
Carpintauto, João Timóteo and Maria Torrada (CCB)
Daniel Avram, Vincent Grama, Grégoire Laroche-Joubert and Jean Michel (arc en rêve)
Kurt Geraerts and Piet Snoeks (Z33)

Contributors
St Crispin's School, Wokingham (United Kingdom)
Lycée agricole François-Pétrarque, Avignon (France)
Geschwister-Scholl-Gesamtschule, Lünen (Germany)
Conservatório de Música Calouste Gulbenkian, Aveiro (Portugal)
Lycée professionnel Jean-Mermoz, Béziers (France)

Akademie der Künste, Berlin
Canadian Centre for Architecture, Montreal
Cité de l'architecture et du patrimoine, Paris
Faculdade de Arquitectura da Universidade do Porto, Porto
UCL Library, London

ARX Portugal Arquitectos, Lisbon
Bak Gordon Arquitectos, Lisbon
Die Baupiloten, Berlin
Manuel Fernandes de Sá, Porto
Foster + Partners, London
Célia Gomes + Machado Costa Arquitectos Associados, Lisbon
Studio Anna Heringer, Laufen
HK Architekten + Florian Nagler Architekten, Schwarzach
Kéré Architecture, Berlin
LIAG Architects and engineers, The Hague
Inês Lobo Arquitectos, Lisbon
Michael Maltzan Architecture, Los Angeles
OFFICE KGVDS, Brussels
3XN Architects, Copenhagen
Wolff Architects, Cape Town
XDGA – Xaveer De Geyter Architects, Brussels

The project received support from the European Education and Culture Executive Agency in the framework of the Europe Creative 2021 programme

Published by
Centro Cultural de Belém / Garagem Sul Architecture Centre (Lisbon, Portugal),
arc en rêve centre d'architecture (Bordeaux, France),
Z33 – House for Contemporary Art, Design & Architecture (Hasselt, Belgium)
and Puente editores (Barcelona, Spain)

Graphic design: Studio Thomas Spallek
Proofreading: George Hutton

Printed in Portugal
ISBN: 978-84-127124-8-3
Legal Deposit: B 515-2024
Print: Orgal impressores, Porto

PUENTE EDITORES

Classroom, a teenage view is a project organised by arc en rêve centre d'architecture (Bordeaux), Centro Cultural de Belém / Garagem Sul Architecture Centre (Lisbon) and Z33 House for Contemporary Art, Design & Architecture (Hasselt). This project is co-funded by the European Union.